CHERISH THE WORD

CHERISH THE WORD

Reflections on Luther's Spirituality

THOMAS C. PETERS

SAINT LOUIS

To
Charlsie and Marijane
Solid Rocks in the Raging Sea

All Scripture quotations, unless otherwise indicated, are taken from the HOLY BIBLE, NEW INTERNATIONAL VERSION®. NIV®. Copyright © 1973, 1978, 1984 by International Bible Society. Used by permission of Zondervan Publishing House. All rights reserved.

Quotations from *Sermons of Martin Luther*. "The House Postils," 3 volumes (ed. by Eugene F. A. Klug; Grand Rapids: Baker Books, 1996) are used by permission of Baker Book House, Co., Grand Rapids, Michigan 49516.

Hymns, prayers, and liturgical materials are taken from *Lutheran Worship* © 1982 by Concordia Publishing House.

Copyright © 2000 Thomas C. Peters
Published by Concordia Publishing House
3558 S. Jefferson Avenue, St. Louis, MO 63118-3968
Manufactured in the United States of America

Library of Congress Cataloging-in-Publication Data

Peters, Thomas C., 1948-
  Cherish the Word : reflections on Luther's spirituality / Thomas C. Peters.
    p. cm.
  ISBN 0-570-05252-1
    1. Spiritual life—Meditations. 2. Spiritual life—Lutheran Church.
  3. Luther, Martin, 1483–1546. Hauspostille. I. Title.
  BV4501.2P48 2000
  248.4′842—dc21   00-009999

1 2 3 4 5 6 7 8 9 10   09 08 07 06 05 04 03 02 01 00

CONTENTS

INTRODUCTION

Much has been said about the momentous material and cultural changes that have taken place during the five hundred years following the life and times of Martin Luther. Since the great reformer re-awakened the Christian world to Scriptures, the central importance of Christ, faith and the holy, the western societies have indeed witnessed profound changes in the political, economic, and social realms. Yet some of the things most essential for the well-being of individual men and women have remained the same; these are the things of the heart.

We are all familiar with those unforgettable words in Ecclesiastes 1:9: "What has been will be again, what has been done will be done again; there is nothing new under the sun." How can biblical wisdom claim that there is nothing new, when in our own lifetime we have seen so many marvels of scientific knowledge and technology? The answer is that the author was not speaking about the peripherals like our artifacts and technology, but rather about the enduring realities of sin, faith and the condition of our hearts and souls. In this sense there is nothing new under the sun. From beginning to end the hearts of fallen humanity are corrupted and in dire need of redemption. Through the centuries the stage settings and the actors may change, but the central drama of sin and redemption remains unchanged.

Of more immediate concern here is the fate of the Christian church since Luther's times. The visible institutions of the Western church have certainly changed—through the Reformation and the proliferation of the Protestant churches, and through the Counter-Reformation and the subsequent reforms in the Roman Catholic Church. But one needs only to read the sermons of Martin Luther to realize that the age-old war over human souls rages on as always. As we reflect on Luther's insights into Scripture and the human condition we see that the issues for individual Christians remain the same. The struggles in the hearts of the faithful today are essentially the same as the struggles of Abraham, Job, David, the prophets, the apostles, and later Martin Luther and the other reformers.

Here we study the homilies of Martin Luther because in them we find the wisdom, the clarity, and the courage that brought about the much-needed reforms in the Christian church and the life of faith. As we remember these great events in history, however, we tend to overlook the fact that Martin Luther's daily existence was that of a local minister. Luther was the pastor of a small flock of Christians in his hometown of Wittenberg, Germany. He was also a family man, and his widespread fame did not cause him to neglect his important responsibilities to his wife and children. The Luther household was said to have been always full of children and guests, and many of Martin Luther's most memorable homilies came from those intimate family times around the hearth and fire.

These Bible-based meditations are designed to explore the basic pastoral thoughts and spiritual insights of Martin Luther. Each chapter features one of Luther's sermons, noting its source after the opening Scripture passage. Each can be read independently; this feature renders the book a resource for personal devotions, leadership training, small-group Bible studies, and Sunday morning Bible study.

There are many compelling reasons for reading and reflecting on Martin Luther's homilies today. The primary reason is that Luther's sermons always begin with a passage of

Scripture, and then proceed to explain and expand from that solid beginning. As a Doctor of Theology and a major figure in the Reformation, Luther provides instruction and insight that speaks to the very core of what Christian doctrine is about. His words are relevant not only for Lutherans, but for Christians of all denominations who accept the basic tenets of Reformation theology.

Another reason to ponder Luther's homilies is that they speak so directly to the conditions of our everyday lives. In reading the works of the various great Christian writers of the past, one is struck by the extraordinary clarity and simplicity with which Luther conveys even profound matters of theology. Just as Luther sought to make the Word of God accessible to the people by translating the Bible into their common language, so in his sermons did he seek to communicate the Word to all who could listen and think.

The quotations included here are taken from the three volumes of the House Postils in *Sermons of Martin Luther* (ed. and trans. by Eugene Klug; Grand Rapids, MI: Baker Book House, 1996). In the preface to these volumes the editor explains that the House Postils are sermons that "were delivered by Luther in the intimate circle of his family members and a few others." Thus these homilies tend to be less formal and yet more concise, showing a greater concern for simplicity of explanation than do the sermons collected in the Church Postils. For this reason these House Postils provide a wellspring of insight and application to our personal walk of faith.

A final word concerns the guiding purpose behind this book. Keep in mind that throughout these chapters—and especially in the journal section "My Reflections"—the desired objective consists in heart work, above and beyond the obvious headwork. We want to move beyond the merely cognitive search for the "right" answer. The goal here is not simply for Christians to come to comfortable agreements on what the answers are; instead, it is for each of us to examine our heart in the light of God's law and through the Spirit of God to draw closer to Christ and His Good News.

As such, our desire is to go beyond the usual level of thinking *about* the topics in this study, and to reach out toward the things of the heart—the things that matter very much to us, perhaps that we feel strongly about. The questions may help you to reflect seriously—perhaps discuss seriously with a friend or friends—your own faith life. The Scripture portions will draw you to the Lord who speaks to His people today through His Word. The objective is to let the Word of God speak to us anew through study, reflection and prayer. Keep in mind that our ultimate goal is to open our hearts and to listen to God as He reveals Himself in Christ Jesus our Lord.

If these objectives and goals seem somewhat ambitious or perhaps unrealistic, it is only because we have forgotten that our Lord desires and expects no less of us. As the Apostle Paul so often urges us, we are called to go deeper into "the hidden wisdom" that is understood only through the gracious gift of the Spirit of God (see for example 1 Corinthians 2:1–16). Generally speaking, we do not go deeper by talking *about* the things of God, but rather by talking directly *with* God, or better, responding to God's Word in faith. Studying the Scriptures, remembering our Baptism into Christ's death and resurrection, thoughtful, meditative prayer, and making a journal to apply God's Word to our lives can be a wonderful way to deepen our understanding and our desire to live in fellowship and discipleship. So, come, let us open our hearts to the Word of God, as we join the great reformer in his home and follow his lead through the basic foundations of our faith.

CHERISH THE WORD

1

LISTEN FOR THE
SHEPHERD'S VOICE

*We seek the voice of our Lord Jesus
and take comfort in His gracious promises.*

"I am the good shepherd. The good shepherd lays down His life for the sheep. The hired hand is not the shepherd who owns the sheep. So when he sees the wolf coming, he abandons the sheep and runs away. Then the wolf attacks the flock and scatters it. The man runs away because he is a hired hand and cares nothing for the sheep.

I am the good shepherd; I know My sheep and My sheep know me—just as the Father knows Me and I know the Father—and I lay down My life for the sheep. I have other sheep that are not of this sheep pen. I must bring them also, and there shall be one flock and one shepherd. (John 10:11–16)

Staring into the screen of my Power Mac, I watch the code words and bar graph as my e-mail message shoots through the modem and then off at the speed of electrons to Chicago some 1,700 miles away. I'm thinking about the Communications Revolution, as we in the more affluent parts of the world witness the continuous development of new electronic media— including e-mail, the world-wide web, satellite television, cellular telephones, and other marvelous technologies.

As is true with every new technology, each innovation brings with it the potential of being used for good or for ill purposes. The advent of television showed us clearly how a mass medium can disseminate both wonders and garbage. And now again, the world to be found under "http://www" demonstrates anew the dual nature of unlimited communications.

On my computer I open my favorite search engine and enter a simple word traditionally related to innocent pleasures. As an experiment I click rapid-fire through the listed sites. There on my screen flash images ranging from a family picnic at a mountain lake to lurid pictures of masochistic sex. It's all there at the command of my fingertips in a matter of seconds.

It is hard not to find these examples of instantaneous media pretty impressive. In fact, as the new technologies amaze the mind, there is a strong tendency to praise the medium and overlook the message. In 1964 a scholar named Marshall McLuhan proclaimed that the human psyche itself had been projected into the electronic media to such an extent that personal identity was no longer tenable. In a sense, he saw the mass media as an expression of the minds of the public. Thus, the medium became the message. We can recognize McLuhan's thesis as an exaggeration at best, but we do find ample reason to heed the warning about the media and our minds.

My random, repeated clicking of the mouse has been too fast for my computer's processor to handle, so the speaker delivers a warning beep and utters a pre-set statement: "Got a problem here," says a human-sounding voice.

There is no question that today we hear more "voices" than ever before. In both a symbolic and a literal sense, various electronic media have rapidly multiplied the "messages" that find their way into our minds. Furthermore, as the advertising industry illustrates, a great number of thoughts, urges, desires, and even perspectives and values are introduced to us subliminally—that is, without our even being aware of the fact.

Among these myriad competing voices, which voice will we hear and follow? If we fail to discern among the voices carefully, we can be deceived with alarming ease. Satan has always loved to fool the faithful, and never has the deception come so easily as now in the age of electronic mass communications. The problem affects not only the secular media; the various cults and even the churches are riddled with errors and falsehoods, and these too are attractively packaged in every kind of popular media. Consequently, discerning the true Shepherd's voice is now more difficult than ever before.

What is the solution? Can my computer give me the answer? No, this Power Mac may be a pretty amazing machine, but in the end it can only deliver what people have put into its memory. We can, however, find the answer in Martin Luther's homily on the Good Shepherd (John 10). He says that it is the responsibility of every Christian to learn—and to keep learning—as much as possible about the Word of God. Discerning the voice of our Shepherd among the noise of our daily lives is not a mere extra for the "spiritually advanced." No, Luther says, our very survival depends upon our recognizing the voice of Christ among the competing voices all around us.

Luther uses Jesus' sermon on the Good Shepherd to encourage us in our faith. Here Luther develops two aspects of the relationship between our Shepherd Jesus and His flock, His sheep: how He recognizes us and how we recognize Him. First is Jesus' "most gracious promise" that no matter how we may doubt, how cold and distant we may feel, or how badly things may seem to go for us, Jesus will never desert us. When we are tempted to doubt this promise, says Luther, we must reply:

> I am certain that He knows me, and even though I must suffer death and all kinds of misfortune, I will not let that thwart my faith; I know and hear and stay close to His voice! For even as a shepherd tenderly calls His little sheep, so Christ also encourages me: I am your shep-

herd, I have laid down My life for you, I died for you! This is the Word I hear and believe. This is my one sure guarantee that He knows me and I know Him. (Second Sunday after Easter, vol. 2, p. 76)

When our feelings betray us, in faith we will say, "Jesus knows me; this I will believe."

Here is a key to Christian faith. In this life everyone is troubled by doubts. Every Christian will at some time or another experience a feeling of having been rejected or abandoned by God. Of course, Satan is always happy to encourage such thoughts and feelings, as clearly illustrated in the Old Testament book of Job. But the meaning of faith, says Luther, is that we nevertheless hold on to the promises of God's Word; we refuse to call God a liar. God has promised that the Shepherd knows His sheep.

The second important issue in Luther's homily is that the sheep must learn to recognize the Shepherd's voice. Luther explains:

That's exactly how it is with a little sheep; its very life depends upon hearing. If it doesn't hear the shepherd's voice, the wolves will soon be there. Without the shepherd's voice, all joy and assurance vanish and only fear and trembling remain. That's how it is also with a Christian: if he loses the Word, all comfort is gone; as long as he is faithful to the Word, he will behold Christ, his shepherd, and therewith everything Christ has earned and promised him, namely, forgiveness of sins and eternal life. (Second Sunday after Easter, vol. 2, p. 77)

Notice how Luther equates the Shepherd's voice with the Word of God. Luther is always very clear in insisting that it is the Word—and not our own goodness and efforts—that sustains us in our life of faith.

"Recognizing a true Christian, therefore, involves far more than outward appearances" says Luther. It's a "matter of hearing the Word." In the sermon Jesus said that the sheep can distinguish their Shepherd's voice from all others. Luther writes, "With this He wants to teach us that if we wish to be Christ's sheep, we must have acute ears, ears that distinguish Christ's voice from all others, regardless how clear, beautiful, enticing, and friendly they may be" (73–74). It is of greatest importance that Christians distinguish the true Word of God from the words of human beings, no matter how important or brilliant or godly those men or women may appear to be.

Here Luther lays the foundation for the Reformation's insistence that the Scriptures must always remain the final authority in matters of the faith. Thus, any other expressions—such as church doctrines, theologies, or sermons—claiming to be God's Word are always subject to the authority of the Scriptures. The Lord's sheep recognize the voice of their Shepherd only, and they listen to no other voice but His.

Such discernment is not as easy as we may at first imagine. Yet Luther gives us sound, practical guidance. The first thing, he says, is to hold on to the assurance that Jesus is always there for us. Then Luther says to cling to the Word—the written Word in the Bible, the spoken Word in gospel sermons, and the Word remembered and pondered at the prompting of the Holy Spirit. Such discernment requires daily times with the Scriptures, meditation, and prayer. To neglect these times is to turn a deaf ear to the voice of the good Shepherd, even as our minds are filled with the other voices that compete incessantly for our attention and loyalties.

At my computer I use the mouse to highlight and click the "Shut Down" command. I've heard enough from the worldwide web for now. Again the speaker beeps, and the screen displays a warning message: "Do you really want to do this?"

In this case, my response is *yes*. Far more important, however, is my response in faith to Christ my Lord. I seek to listen to His voice. I gladly hear His promises to me.

Cherishing the Word

1. What is the "most gracious promise" that our Lord Jesus makes to His flock?

2. Luther encourages us to hear and trust our Shepherd's voice faithfully. What does it mean to be faithful to the Word?

3. The Pharisees studied the Scriptures diligently, yet they could not hear the Word because they refused to believe in Christ (John 5:39–40). How, then, can we prepare ourselves to hear God's Word?

> We are to be such little sheep and not only hear our shepherd's voice, the voice of the Lord Jesus, but follow it faithfully and alone. Christ's voice says to us, You are a poor sinner, but I died for your sins; by clinging to Me you will be saved. We should listen to that and follow Him, always believing: That is my shepherd's voice. (Second Sunday after Easter, vol. 2, p. 74)

• Do I daily hear my Shepherd speak to me? How can I develop my ability to listen and to hear God's call to me each day?

• Who or what are the "wolves" in my life—those things that would destroy my soul if I did not hear and follow the voice of my Shepherd?

• What exactly can I say to myself at times when I am tempted to feel that God has deserted me?

• What insights or blessings would I like to share with others?

> My sheep listen to My voice; I know them, and they follow Me. I give them eternal life, and they shall never perish; no one can snatch them out of My hand. My Father, who has given them to Me, is greater than all; no one can snatch them out of My Father's hand. (John 10:27–29)

Reflections

2

GOD REALLY FORGIVES OUR SINS

As we recognize and confess our sins, we know the comfort of God's gracious forgiveness.

While they were still talking about this, Jesus Himself stood among them and said to them, "Peace be with you."

They were startled and frightened, thinking they saw a ghost. He said to them, "Why are you troubled, and why do doubts rise in your minds? Look at My hands and My feet. It is I Myself! Touch Me and see; a ghost does not have flesh and bones, as you see I have."

When He had said this, He showed them His hands and feet. And while they still did not believe it because of joy and amazement, He asked them, "Do you have anything here to eat?" They gave Him a piece of broiled fish, and He took it and ate it in their presence.

He said to them, "This is what I told you while I was still with you: Everything must be fulfilled that is written about Me in the Law of Moses, the prophets and the Psalms."

> Then He opened their minds so they could understand the Scriptures. He told them, "This is what is written: The Christ will suffer and rise from the dead on the third day, and repentance and forgiveness of sins will be preached in His name to all nations, beginning at Jerusalem. (Luke 24:36–47)

When I was in graduate school, "pop psychology" was the rage. It seemed that everyone was reading books by Fritz Perls, Carl Rogers, Abraham Maslow and Eric Berne, and almost everyone was going to some kind of group therapy sessions. As a self-styled "open-minded" intellectual, I was no exception.

One of the great things I discovered about therapy groups was that people seemed to listen and take me seriously. I found that the group's attention to me and my problems made me feel somewhat special and important, if even for those brief moments in that circumscribed time and place. On the other hand, I couldn't help but notice the strong biases toward self-centeredness and irresponsibility in the flow of the therapy. It seemed that everyone's "cure" lay in breaking with some tradition, reneging on some agreement or vow, or asserting one's personal rights regardless of the consequences for others. The very idea of "right and wrong" was considered laughable, submission or service to others was definitely suspect, and "guilt" was declared the number one destructive relic of our repressive past. "Guilt is baloney!" my therapist liked to proclaim at the appropriate moment.

Guilt has indeed gone out of style, and most people today would bid it a hearty good riddance. I think that many of us, Christian and non-Christian alike, would prefer simply to dismiss our feelings of guilt and never give them another thought. Luther, however, reminds us that mere denial and dismissal accomplish nothing in the eternally real matters of sin and guilt. True, Christians are certainly not to live under a perennial load of guilt feelings, but our guilt doesn't disappear just because we unilaterally declare that guilt is baloney.

We Christians know that we feel guilty because we are guilty. In this sense our feelings of guilt are a legitimate tool used by the Holy Spirit to get our attention and ultimately drive us to Christ. When we simply dismiss our feelings of guilt without examining ourselves and recognizing our shortcomings and crimes, we miss a great opportunity to unburden ourselves from the formidable load of real sins. Here is the path of self-justification and false righteousness, a lamentable habit that plagues us all.

Perhaps like most people, I have a hard time admitting my guilt. Sure, in the abstract I can magnanimously concede that I'm not perfect, that I make mistakes, and even that I'm included in the verdict of Romans 3:23. But confessing specific, particular, concrete instances of my sin can be a pretty big pill to swallow. I'd much rather dodge the issue by proclaiming that guilt is baloney, or making excuses, or blaming someone or something else, or claiming my rights. However, Luther's homily brings me right back to the essential point: The life of faith summons me to face my sin squarely and to confess it to my Lord.

In his homily on Luke 24:36–47 Martin Luther elaborates on the appearance of the resurrected Jesus to the disciples in hiding. Jesus' purpose in appearing was meant not to frighten His followers, but to give them the peace and reassurance they so dearly needed. Though these men had deserted Jesus in His time of peril and had even denied knowing Him, the risen Lord still came back to comfort them and "open their eyes" to the grace of God's forgiveness.

So it is with us as well. Like the twelve disciples, we fail our Lord and continue to sin. Luther says:

> So a Christian is at the same time sinner and saint. As persons, we are sinful by nature and in our own name are sinners. But Christ marks us with another name, forgiveness of sins. For His sake our sins are remitted and taken away. So both are true: Sins are there, because the "Old Adam" is not dead yet; and they are not there,

because God for Christ's sake will not look at them. They are before my eyes, I see them and feel them only too well; but there is Christ commanding me to repent, that is to confess myself a sinner, be converted, and believe in the forgiveness of sins in His name. (Easter Tuesday, vol. 2, p. 39)

As long as we remain in these mortal bodies, we shall continue to be dogged by our sins. Luther says that because Christ wants the whole world to come to repentance, "there is no person on earth who in his mind is to be excused or excepted, but must confess and acknowledge that they are sinners" (36).

If in our pride we refuse to acknowledge our sins, it follows that we thereby deprive ourselves of the Lord's forgiveness and comfort. Luther explains, "How to become a Christian, must in every case be to confess our sins, for otherwise you can neither rejoice in your forgiveness nor be comforted" (36). Thus our own arrogance and disbelief prevent us from receiving the gift of God's mercy. Our despair results not from God's arbitrary punishment for our mistakes, but from our own deliberate refusal to accept God's forgiveness and comfort.

Here Luther speaks about one of my other bad habits. Once the Spirit has pierced my hard heart and convinced me to confess and repent of my sins, then I sometimes make the grave mistake of holding on to the guilt. Do you have a hard time forgiving yourself sometimes? Saying that God forgives me is one thing, but truly forgiving myself and letting go of the guilty feelings is another. Yet, Luther says that to continue to dwell on my guilt is to reject the gift of God's gracious redemption and, even worse, to call God a liar!

Now, there's a statement that commands my attention. Luther's insights are particularly germane to those "pop psychology" notions about guilt. Yes, Luther would say, I agree that guilt is baloney, but only after the sin has been removed. When you are still living unrepentant in your sins, your guilt feelings are a sign of judgment and an invitation to rid yourself from sin. If your therapy denies the obvious reality and eternal importance of sin, then it merely helps you to avoid the most profound healing you could ever hope to experience.

And for us Christians—I feel as if Luther has found my face among the crowd in his congregation and is speaking directly to me—we must always remember that God is infinitely good and loving. In 1 John 1:9 God has expressly promised complete forgiveness of our confessed sins. Will we look such a loving God in the face and say, "I don't believe You"? The invitation is open: Cast your guilt into the sea of God's mercy, and claim your freedom from the bondage of guilt for your sins.

The good news of the Gospel, says Luther, is that in Jesus' death, burial and resurrection our sins are forgiven. When we confess our sins and receive God's grace through faith we have life and salvation. Luther writes:

> Well, what are we to do? Should we therefore despair because we are sinners, knowing that God is the enemy of sin? No, on the contrary, because forgiveness of sins is to be preached with repentance, and we are to proclaim forgiveness of sins in Christ's name to all who hear and believe, therefore receive it and be comforted, saying, Lord, I am a sinner, but spare me; I will live by grace alone, which is offered to me in Your name. This is the way to go and you are saved. This is preaching forgiveness in Christ's name. All who accept the gospel and believe on Christ have their sins wiped away. Without Christ there is no forgiveness; but in Christ there is nothing but forgiveness. (Easter Tuesday, vol. 2, p. 37)

Christ requires not only that we repent, but furthermore that we believe that we are forgiven. Many are aware of their own sins, fewer are sorry for them, and even fewer still are able to believe that their sins are forgiven and forgotten. Those who through faith accept the forgiveness of sins, says Luther, are the true Christians.

Notice here the narrow way that treads carefully between arrogance and despair. To deny our sins is merely to add arrogance to our growing list of sins. On the other hand, to refuse

God's forgiveness—that is, to hang onto our feelings of guilt over confessed sins—is the sin of unbelief and the sure road to utter despair.

> But we ought to thank God that we have come to grace, have confessed ourselves sinners, and can comfort ourselves with God's grace, and consequently in this grace perform genuine good works which go along with repentance and faith. For wherever this doctrine and and preaching are found, Christ will be also, and no devil will approach. So there is no need to fear the devil anymore, or be afraid of him. For instead there is forgiveness of sins and a merry, peaceful heart, which does gladly all that it ought to do. (vol. 2, p. 38)

We are indeed sinners, because we are human. We are indeed saints, because we confess our sins to God our Father and believe in His only Son, Christ our Lord. We Christians surely have cause for deep humility, but we surely have cause for great joy as well! The thought of such a promise humbles me, and I thank God that I can now say so much more than, "Guilt is baloney."

I say, Christ is my hope, my comfort, my Savior.

ALL GLORY BE TO GOD ALONE

All glory be to God alone,
  Forevermore the Highest One.
He is our sinful race's friend;
  His grace and peace to us extend.
May humankind see His goodwill,
  May hearts with deep thanksgiving fill.

We praise You, God; Your name we bless
  And worship You in humbleness;
From day to day we glorify
  Our everlasting God on high.
Your splendor's glorious light we sing,
  And to Your throne our thanks we bring.

Lord God, our King on heaven's throne,
  Our Father, the Almighty One.
O Lord, the Sole-begotten One,
  Lord Jesus Christ, the Father's Son,
True God for all eternity,
  O Lamb of God, to you we flee.

You take the whole world's sin away;
  Have mercy on us, Lord, we pray.
You take the whole world's sin away;
  Oh, listen to the prayer we say.
From God's right hand, oh, sent today
  Your mercy on us, Lord, we pray.

You are the only Holy One,
  The Lord of all things, You alone.
O Jesus Christ, we glorify You
  and the Spirit, Lord Most High;
With Him You evermore will be
  One in the Father's majesty.

—Martin Luther (attributed)

27

Cherishing the Word

1. How does the Christian way of faith resemble a narrow path that runs between arrogance and despair?

2. Why is refusal to forgive oneself a matter of disbelief?

3. How can the weaknesses and failings of Jesus' twelve disciples serve to encourage us in our faith?

> Then learn to build upon God's grace, looking to Jesus' name, in which forgiveness of sins is preached. He who believes this, sin cannot harm. For forgiveness of sins is greater than all sins; it goes far beyond all sin, and is mightier and stronger than all sin. Therefore, sin cannot harm the one who is in Christ and has forgiveness of sins in His name. As for forgiveness, it is not earned but is a gift by grace. So we are righteous, not as though we had no sin, but because, for Christ's sake, by grace, we are counted righteous by God.... (Easter Tuesday, vol. 2, p. 40)

- Do I sometimes have a hard time forgiving myself or others? What useful instruction can I take from Luther's words?

- What is the significance to me—personally—of Jesus' reassuring appearance to the disciples who had deserted him?

- My prayer—confession, petition, or praise—to God about His gracious forgiveness in Christ.

- What insights or blessings would I like to share with others?

> If we claim to be without sin, we deceive ourselves and the truth is not in us. If we confess our sins, He is faithful and just and will forgive us our sins and purify us from all unrighteousness. (1 John 1:8–9)

Reflections

3

FAITH ALONE

We celebrate our faith in Christ
and know His power for daily life.

Then He got into the boat and His disciples followed
Him. Without warning, a furious storm came up on the
lake, so that the waves swept over the boat. But Jesus
was sleeping. The disciples went and woke Him saying,
"Lord, save us! We're going to drown!"

He replied, "You of little faith, why are you so afraid?"
Then He got up and rebuked the winds and the waves,
and it was completely calm.

The men were amazed and asked, "What kind of man is
this? Even the winds and the waves obey Him!"
(Matthew 8:23–27)

The radio in my car is turned up loud, as my teenage son,
Sam, and I leave the city and head south on the interstate
freeway. A man on the "oldies" station sings about the need to
be good, because he wants to see his baby when he leaves this
world.

Remember that one? While I drive and reminisce, my
mind drifts back to Martin Luther's comments on faith alone.

It isn't only old rock and roll songs that labor under the misconception that the way to Heaven is to "be good." This idea is probably one of the most widely held beliefs among ordinary people in traditionally Christian countries even today. A great many church-going folk also talk about being good so they can go to Heaven—or at least that's what they say to their children. But even more telling are the well-versed Christians who like to say "faith alone," but then act as if their church attendance and offerings are their ticket to Heaven.

Luther's homily on Matthew 8:23–27 is one of his many fine sermons on the characteristics and benefits of faith. Using the Gospel episode where Jesus calms the raging sea, Luther derives four lessons of value to us in our everyday walk in the Christian faith.

The first truth concerns the storm itself. The sea was calm and benign before Jesus entered the boat, but then afterward it became a threatening storm. Luther equates this tumult to the rancor of Satan whenever a person follows Christ.

> As soon as the teaching about faith is in the picture and Christ steps into the ship, then, as the saying goes, It won't be long before there's threatening weather; the sun won't shine any longer and the sea will rage and storm.... This all works together, if you want to be a Christian and follow this Lord, and step with Him into the ship, resigning your heart to Him and composing your soul in patience. For as soon as you commit your-self to this Lord and come with Him into the ship wind, storm, and buffeting will surely ensue.... But don't despair ... do not be afraid because of that, but think rather: I didn't get into this to gain the world's favor; and I'm not going to give it up because of its rancor and raging. (Fourth Sunday after Epiphany, vol. 1, p. 254)

Christians should expect persecution; we may be ridiculed for our faith, discriminated against, harassed, mistreated, tormented and, in some countries today, killed. Only in Christ can we weather these many assaults with faith and courage.

Luther's second point is about the right "shape" of faith. The sinking sailors had done everything in their power to save themselves, but it availed nothing against the raging sea. Weak as their faith was, however, it was indeed their faith in Jesus that prompted them to cry, "Save us!" When everything seems to be going well, Luther points out, we think our own efforts can accomplish anything. Against the powers of Satan, sin and death, however, we quickly discover how utterly powerless we really are.

Here is the meaning of Luther's famous axiom that it is "faith alone" that makes salvation our own. In Luther's time the Church taught that salvation could be merited by various human works, including such things as monastic vows, pilgrimages, acts of penance, and even the purchase of indulgences. Though these are not the kinds of "works" that seem relevant to us today, there is still a widespread notion—even among Christians—that certain kinds of moral piety are sufficient to merit righteousness and God's favor.

As I drive among the traffic on the freeway, I'm thinking about the Reformation. Luther was always clear on not only the proper role of works in our salvation, but also about the nature of good works. He insisted that good works are a sign that one's faith is alive and well. And by good works he always meant useful works of charity toward the people in our lives. To Luther, pilgrimages, relics, repetitious rituals, and self-appointed acts of piety were offensive precisely because they served as substitutes for good, useful works for people in need. The issue was doing religious-looking things instead of acts of charity. Commenting on the Galilean storm, Luther says:

> The disciples in the ship had a weak faith; nevertheless, they sought help where it was to be found, namely, with the Lord Jesus; they awoke Him and cried, "Lord, save us, we perish!"

> The Lord described them as men of little faith; but He acknowledged that they had faith, though small and weak. If they had not faith, they would not have awak-

ened Christ in their need. But the fact that they did awaken Him is evidence of faith. For no one can call upon God, especially in a crisis, unless he has faith. Even though there was but a spark of faith in the disciples, it shone forth and clung to the person who could overpower death. (Fourth Sunday after Epiphany, vol. 1, p. 259)

The shape of genuine faith, then, comes down to one simple cry, "Lord, help!" It is the posture and desperate appeal of a needy, perishing soul.

As Sam and I speed along the freeway at seventy miles per hour, suddenly we find ourselves trapped behind a slow-moving truck, in front of an aggressive tailgater, between a steady stream of cars on the left and a merging bus on the right. There is no place to go. I straddle the lane marker and brace for the honking and screeching of tires, or worse.

"God, help us!" I am thinking.

"Lord, save us, we perish!" Luther quoted the disciples in his sermon. This statement, said Luther, is the essence of the Christian faith. After our crisis on the freeway passes without injury, I reflect on Luther's meaning. There is certainly no trace of pride, arrogance, smugness or self-righteousness in such a cry for deliverance. Luther reminds us that we sin daily, and we therefore need to humble ourselves and plead for God's help every day.

The third lesson that Luther finds in the story is a strong affirmation that Jesus Christ is both man and God, as the Church's creeds assert. For as a man Jesus needed sleep, but as God He calmed the waves of the sea. In this knowledge we ought to find comfort, for as Luther says:

The fact is that when He threatens the sea and the wind, and they obey Him, this proves His almighty Godhead, that He is the Lord over the sea and wind. With one word He can quiet the sea and cause the wind to abate. This is not the work of mere man. The power of God is needed to control the violence of the sea with one word. Christ, therefore, is not only a natural man, but truly God.... For Christ, true God and true man, helps all those who believe in Him and call upon Him in every time of need and danger. (Fourth Sunday after Epiphany, vol. 1, pp. 261–62)

Because He is fully human and divine, Jesus understands our afflictions; in mercy He helps us to overcome hardship and fear.

Finally, Luther speaks of the fruits that result from having faith in times of trouble. Faithful Christians know that their troubles will lead to blessing under God's hand. The Reformer admits frankly that Christians are in for more than their share of trouble, but faith clings to the promise that God will bring us through affliction according to His goodness in Christ.

Sam asks if he can change the setting on the radio, and I somewhat reluctantly agree. Perhaps predictably, our tastes in music differ greatly. When he finds his preferred station, I hear a rock group called Big Tent Revival singing about God making our faith grow, just as water and sunshine make a little seed grow.

These lyrics sound good to me, and I'm certainly grateful that my son prefers Christian rock to something like "gangster rap." I feel humbled and yet grateful to realize that Sam's music contains such wisdom, even if my "oldies" contain much foolishness.

Luther's homily is a message of wisdom—God's wisdom—for the church. We possess a prideful propensity to flaunt our piety and to imagine we're doing God a great favor with our good works. Yet the pages of both the Old and the New Testament virtually shout the warning to us that God deplores such religious pride. Luther reiterates that what our Father wants is our faith alone—our simple, humble, patient faith in Christ, His mercy, His good gifts. This faith is the kind that waits on the Lord and cries, "Lord, save us, we perish!"

Cherishing the Word

1. Why does it sometimes seem that committed Christians suffer more adversity than others do?

2. Why does Luther lay such great importance in the thought that we are saved through "faith alone"?

3. What should be our attitude as Christians toward our troubles and afflictions?

> If you wish to be a Christian, you will certainly experience trials. However, if you call upon Christ in time of need, He will hear you, rescue you, and cause your trial to bear blessed fruit and great glory. (Fourth Sunday after Epiphany, vol. 1, p. 263)

- Have I unintentionally allowed notions of "works righteousness" to slip into my life? Do the things I do at church make me feel that I am earning favor with God? Do I find subtle ego rewards at my church? Do I derive a secret pride in my pious acts?

- Do I have a hard time not trying to control everything in my life? What are some areas where I might improve my walk of faith by saying, "Lord, help!"?

- How can Jesus' humanity—His temptations, His suffering, His disappointments and sorrows—help me to trust in His caring love in my own hard times?

- What insights or blessings would I like to share with others?

> But now a righteousness from God, apart from law, has been made known, to which the Law and the Prophets testify. This righteousness from God comes through faith in Jesus Christ to all who believe. There is no difference, for all have sinned and fall short of the glory of God, and are justified freely by His grace through the redemption that came by Christ Jesus. (Romans 3:21–24)

Reflections

THE APOSTLES' CREED

The Second Article with Explanation

I believe in Jesus Christ, His only Son, our Lord, who was conceived by the Holy Spirit, born of the Virgin Mary, suffered under Pontius Pilate, was crucified, died and was buried. He descended into hell. The third day He rose again from the dead. He ascended into heaven and sits at the right hand of God the Father Almighty. From thence He will come to judge the living and the dead.

What does this mean? I believe that Jesus Christ, true God, begotten of the Father from eternity, and also true man, born of the Virgin Mary, is my Lord,

who has redeemed me, a lost and condemned person, purchased and won me from all sins, from death, and from the power of the devil; not with gold or silver, but with His holy, precious blood and with His innocent suffering and death,

that I may be His own and live under Him in His kingdom, and serve Him in everlasting righteousness, innocence, and blessedness,

just as He is risen from the dead, lives and reigns to all eternity.

This is most certainly true.

—*Martin Luther (1529)*

4

WORK ... BUT DON'T WORRY

*In faith, we see the grace of God's providence
and personal care for daily life.*

No one can serve two masters. Either he will hate the
one and love the other, or he will be devoted to the one
and despise the other. You cannot serve both God and
Money.

Therefore I tell you, do not worry about your life, what
you will eat or drink; or about your body, what you will
wear. Is not life more important than food, and the
body more important than clothes? Look at the birds of
the air; they do not sow or reap or store away in barns,
and yet Your heavenly Father feeds them. Are you not
much more valuable than they? Who of you by worrying can add a single hour to his life?

And why do you worry about clothes? See how the lilies
of the field grow. They do not labor or spin. Yet I tell
you that not even Solomon in all his splendor was
dressed like one of these. If that is how God clothes the
grass of the field, which is here today and tomorrow is
thrown into the fire, will He not much more clothe you,

O you of little faith? So do not worry, saying, "What shall we eat?" or "What shall we drink?" or "What shall we wear?" for the pagans run after all these things, and your heavenly Father knows that you need them. But seek first His kingdom and His righteousness, and all these things will be given to you as well. Therefore do not worry about tomorrow, for tomorrow will worry about itself. Each day has enough trouble of its own. (Matthew 6:24–34)

Sometimes lessons in life seem brutally harsh. But then we also have to admit that we often make it very difficult for God to get our attention. In the Old Testament God called the Israelites "a stiff-necked people." When we are honest, we recognize that the same can be said of us today. Do you remember the popular Frank Sinatra song, "I Did It My Way"? It seems we always want to do everything our own way.

I confess that I've spent most of my adult life trying to control everything around me in such a way that I won't be confronted by unexpected problems, threats, troubles, pains, set-backs or even inconveniences. Of course, I recognize a certain measure of this effort as merely a part of the standard male role of leader, protector, and problem-solver in the family. I recognize as well that control isn't only a male problem; it's a human problem. Women struggle with this issue as much as men do, even if their perspectives and parameters tend to be different. Like Adam and Eve in the primordial garden, we each still grapple daily with the perennial temptation to "be like gods" and conduct our lives as if we're the autonomous masters of our fates.

The last few years, however, have brought me some hard lessons. How many sermons have I heard addressing "God and Mammon" and "the lilies of the field"? How many opportunities have I had to learn this lesson by simply hearing and doing the Word of God? Yet I wasn't really hearing; I really didn't get it. I filled my life with my plans and my efforts to control my surroundings. In a sense I wanted to force the world to treat me and my family the way we wanted to be treated. I had my plans, but God had other plans.

Suddenly without warning, my wife Lynn was struck down with a post-viral, chronic fatigue syndrome. Overnight our income was slashed by half. The adjustments were hard; we had to sell some of our belongings and make other dramatic changes in lifestyle. Then a few years later came the sudden discovery that I had cancer requiring major surgery. Again our income was slashed by almost half, and I wondered—I worried—how we could survive on so little. I believe now that God was teaching us lessons of the greatest value: the lessons of Mammon and God, and of the lilies of the field.

In his homily on Matthew 6:24–34, Luther cites Jesus' sermon about serving two masters, pointing out the impossibility of our serving God while we are busy worrying and fussing about our money and belongings. The Lord's comments on Mammon are today as timely as ever, because our world—perhaps even more than the world in Luther's day—seems completely engulfed in greed.

To his family and friends, Luther proclaimed:

Day and night everybody's greatest concern is how to make a living. And this stimulates greed to the point where no one is content with what God provides and bestows. Everybody wants more and craves moving up the ladder. Whomever God has blessed with a beautiful house covets owning a mansion. If he has a mansion, he then wants a villa with expansive grounds, [and] so is never satisfied. Everyone wants to get on better and have more. If it were not for greed and pride, everybody would have enough and people would not be so concerned about things, scraping and scratching. (Fifteenth Sunday after Trinity, vol. 3, p. 16)

Though Luther spoke these words in the year 1534, they describe very well the perennial discontent underlying our consumerist way of life today. But Luther warns, "Not only is such anxiety needless and useless; it is an obstacle to true worship of God" (16).

Luther's point is that worry and anxiety about money have much to do with a lack of trust in God. If we truly believe that God has given us the wonderful gift of eternal life, he asks, "should we not trust that He will also give us lesser things?" Luther illustrates:

> If a rich man were to give you a thousand pieces of gold—something that would be painful for him to do—wouldn't you trust him to give you a pair of old shoes? This is exactly how we treat our Lord God in heaven when we are anxious about food and drink, since he has already given us the greatest and best. Just think how such anxiety must displease Him. (Fifteenth Sunday after Trinity, vol. 3, p. 17)

Luther hastens to add that Jesus promises that the heavenly Father will provide. If God gives us body and life (and He does), He will also give us food and clothing. If He gives us enough to support ourselves in this life (and He does), is there any reason to be anxious, to fret, to despair? In truth, God provides. Luther concludes, "He doesn't want you to be in need of anything; simply believe that it is true and that He wants to be your God and Father" (17).

What does Jesus' sermon mean? Do the lilies of the field tell us that we can all quit our jobs and be flower children and live off the land? Luther's reply is an emphatic "No." We are to work and do what we can to support and protect our families, but we are not to imagine that we have complete, absolute control over what will happen to us. Luther says to work, but not to worry. If we think that we are the masters of our own destiny, then we worry over every little thing that eludes our efforts. The choice between Mammon and God is ultimately the choice of whether we put trust in ourselves and our things or if we put our trust in God.

Our calling and responsibility as Christians is to work as we can, to be grateful for what we have, and to refrain from greed and worrying. True faith, says Luther, "...works and trusts in God, commending to Him the caring and accepting of what He bestows." Jesus' sermon in the Scripture passage contains an important promise: "But seek first His kingdom and His righteousness, and all these things will be given to you as well" (Matthew 6:33). Luther says we either trust in God's promise, or we call God a liar. "Mammon, you see, permits no trust in God" (21). God's promise is that as we turn our full attention to seeking His kingdom, we have no need to worry about our income and our physical well-being. Faith accepts God's promises as true.

The hardest part of my weeks of recovery from surgery was that I felt completely helpless and dependent. Yet it was during those weeks of pain and uncertainty that I finally began to learn this important lesson of trust. There was no way that I could pretend to be in control; I had no choice but to depend on my wife, family, and God. The illusions were stripped away; I realized that God takes care of business with or without my efforts and worry.

Away from the noise of the workplace and the marketplace, I began to understand what it means to put my trust in God. Another way of saying this is that in withdrawing from Mammon I drew closer to God. For a controlling person like me, trusting is an odd feeling and not an easy thing to accept. But now that I'm back on the job and once again engaged in the push and shove of public life, the challenge lies in whether I can continue to put my trust in God, even as the people and events around me seem to threaten, cajole, seduce, and whisper the old lie: "You can be like a god ... it's time to take control again." These thoughts assault my mind; however, in my heart I know otherwise.

In his homily Luther invites us to stop following the spirit of our age—the ungrateful urge to acquisition, the siren call of the shopping mall, the commercial habit of "scraping and scratching." As children of God, renewed by the Holy Spirit, we daily reflect upon the many things that God has provided for us. Luther concludes:

So, in this Gospel our dear Lord Jesus Christ entices us with beautiful pictures and examples, in order that we learn to trust in God; and He promises that God will give us all we need if we but trust Him and do our work. In fact, God has already demonstrated, and demonstrates every day, that He wants to provide for our needs. Through the earth, the air, and water, He daily bestows His gifts to us human beings.... (Fifteenth Sunday after Trinity, vol. 3, p. 23)

In our ingratitude we have blinded ourselves to the miracles of grace and providence that God showers upon us daily. In our consumer society we let ourselves be mesmerized by the lie that we always need more than what we have. Luther suggests, "Do like the birds—learn to believe, sing, be happy, and let your heavenly Father do the caring for you" (19).

At home my yard doesn't have any lilies in it, but it does have some poppies that delighted me each day of my recovery. And now every morning as I leave for work, those glorious golden flowers remind me of Luther's homily on Jesus' sermon. I say to myself, "Yes, go to work, but let God take care of the worrying."

MORNING PRAYER

I thank You, my heavenly Father, through Jesus Christ, Your dear Son, that You have kept me this night from all harm and danger;

And I pray that You would keep me this day also from sin and every evil, that all my doings and life may please You.

For into Your hands I commend myself, my body and soul, and all things. Let Your holy angel be with me, that the evil foe may have no power over me. Amen.

EVENING PRAYER

I thank You, my heavenly Father, through Jesus Christ, Your dear Son, that You have graciously kept me this day;

And I pray that You would forgive me all my sins where I have done wrong, and graciously keep me this night.

For into Your hands I commend myself, my body and soul, and all things. Let Your holy angel be with me, that the evil foe may have no power over me. Amen.

—*Martin Luther (1529)*

Cherishing the Word

1. What is the relationship between greed and ingratitude? How does this relationship illustrate Jesus' sermon on Mammon and God?

2. Why is our anxiety and worry displeasing to God?

3. What are some of the ways our consumer society seduces us into ungrateful attitudes and vain strivings?

> The kingdom of God, therefore, is nothing else but hearing and believing God's Word. God rules within us when we do not despair of Him, but trust Him wholeheartedly and esteem Him as our God and Father. Where such faith exists, there God dwells, and righteousness immediately follows, that is, forgiveness of sins.(vol. 3, p. 22)

• To what extent am I affected by what other people have, by the symbols of success, by media-created discontent, and by the habitual urge to consume?

• What are some of the many things that God has granted me to which I have blinded myself by my ingratitude? What are some of the great gifts that I have undervalued, and some of the trivial things that I have overvalued?

• My prayer—confession, petition, or praise—to God for His provision.

• What insights or blessings would I like to share with others?

> I thank my God every time I remember you. In all my prayers for all of you, I always pray with joy because of your partnership in the gospel from the first day until now, being confident of this, that He who began a good work in you will carry it on to completion until the day of Christ Jesus. (Philippians 1:3–6)

Reflections

5

BE PATIENT IN ADVERSITY

We focus on God's promises in our troubles.

"In a little while you will see Me no more and then after a little while you will see Me."

Some of His disciples said to one another, "What does He mean by saying, 'In a little while you will see Me no more, and then after a little while you will see Me,' and 'Because I am going to the Father'?" They kept asking, "What does He mean by 'a little while'? We don't understand what He is saying."

Jesus saw that they wanted to ask Him about this, so He said to them, "Are you asking one another what I meant when I said, 'In a little while you will see Me no more, and then after a little while you will see Me'? I tell you the truth, you will weep and mourn while the world rejoices. You will grieve, but your grief will turn to joy! A woman giving birth to a child has pain because her time has come; but when her baby is born she forgets the anguish because of her joy that a child is born into the world. So with you: Now is your time of grief, but I will see you again and you will rejoice, and no one will take away your joy. In that day you will no longer ask Me anything. I tell you the truth, My Father will give you whatever you ask in My name. (John 16:16–23)

I want to offer a tribute to a woman named Charlsie, who could tell us a great deal about adversity and patience. Now a widow in her eighties, she has been a Christian all her life, and she still looks to her Lord Jesus as she patiently endures the losses and frustrations that inevitably come with the final decades of life. Her life hasn't been easy, but the example of her enduring love and patience is the stuff that causes her children and grandchildren to "arise and call her blessed" (Proverbs 31:28).

During the fifty-some years that I've known Charlsie, I've watched her endure poverty, isolation, gossip, rejection, overwork, loss of dreams, and personal challenges of many kinds. I've seen some of her closest friends and relatives turn away from her because of her visible and unyielding faith in Christ. They called her a "religious fanatic" because she never flinched from letting her faith be known to any and every person who came into her life. For over a half-century I've watched her endure innumerable hardships, deprivations and pains; yet, I have never heard her complain about any of them.

Drawing upon Jesus' words that the disciples "weep and mourn while the world rejoices," Martin Luther reminds us in his sermon on John 16:16–23 that we Christians will inevitably suffer hardships, ridicule and more. Luther says:

> It's the same story with us today. We, who confess Christ and His gospel, must bear oppression and tribulation, while on the other hand, our opponents rejoice.... Meanwhile, we have sorrow, pain, suffering, misery, and distress. Our Christ is gone, and we gain nothing from it but the wrangling and exulting of the adversaries....
>
> So it will also be for the disciples, says Christ.... We must weep and mourn while the world laughs, boasts, glories, and mocks us. The Lord told us beforehand that it would happen this way; He has been taken from us, weeping and mourning have darkened our door, but the world is joyful and rejoices. This you should bear in mind and in patience possess your souls, consoling one

another with these words. (Third Sunday after Easter, vol. 2, p. 89)

From these comments it becomes clear that complaining is not a legitimate option for Christians; we are to expect adversity and to bear it patiently, by God's grace and strength.

But how much adversity is a person expected to bear? Shouldn't there be a reasonable limit to the patience required of a Christian? The adversity in Charlsie's life assumed a particularly difficult form, in that her husband wrestled with mental illness for the last thirty years of his life. Through those dark decades of his weeping and wailing, his unpredictable outbursts, and his depressive episodes, his wife endured patiently— like the unmoved rock in a storm at sea—while working to pay the bills and raising four frightened children to adulthood and faith. How could she endure? How could anyone find such patience? Charlsie would be the first to answer that her patience was grounded in her faith and the hope of eternal life.

Indeed, Luther says, a Christian's patience is founded on the bigger picture, the eternal perspective. The Scripture lesson speaks repeatedly of "a little while," reminding us that our trials in our lifetimes are mere fleeting moments in eternity. Furthermore, the bad news is again followed by a gracious promise. If we endure our hardships with patience for a little while, our reward will be joy for eternity. Luther puts it this way:

> The sorrowing of Christians and the rejoicing of the world both have their "little while." Christians will weep and lament; the world, on the other hand, will sing, dance, and celebrate! Be of good cheer, take the pause that refreshes and before you know it, there will be a trade-off: sorrow changing into joy, and joy into sorrow. At the close of this Gospel lesson He [Jesus] says very clearly, "Your heart shall rejoice, and your joy no man taketh from you." In other words, sorrow will finally be transmuted into eternal joy—a joy which no one can ever take from you! (Third Sunday after Easter, vol. 2, p. 89–90)

God's promise is that the pains we suffer now are small compared to the joys we shall have later on. This is the very promise that has nourished Charlsie's patience through many years.

Luther also applies this Gospel to our daily life of faith, urging us not to dwell on our doubts and bad feelings. Christians who focus on self and present circumstances take their eyes off the word of promise. "The more he concentrates on what he feels and how much it hurts," Luther writes of the believer, "the more quickly he will succumb to fright, doubts, and impatience" (94).

We all have known times when our faith seems to go "dry." Our feelings give us no satisfaction that we are indeed God's special children. Again, says Luther, the remedy lies in our patience and hope in the Word. As long as we focus our attention on our own condition, we remain trapped in a cycle of fear, doubts and impatience. When we bring our feelings under control and focus instead on God's promises, then we find the hope and patience to wait for God to keep his Word.

The Lord knows well the human heart and its habits. He knows how self-centered we are prone to be, and how we love to make a great issue of our perceived wrongs and sufferings. He knows how our complaints serve to inflame our feelings, and how our uncontrolled feelings serve to invite our complaints. Nevertheless He calls us to persist in patience and hope in His Word, and He will reward us with his peace and joy. On this note Luther concludes:

> When we thus cling to the Word, persisting patiently in faith and hope, Christ will let us see Him again—exactly as the great sorrow of the disciples was dispelled when they saw Him again after His resurrection. And so let's not dwell too long on our suffering, how much we hurt and how unfair those are who cause the hurt, but instead nurture that happy outlook which depends on Christ's pledge, "I will see you again and your heart shall rejoice, and your joy no man taketh from you." (Third Sunday after Easter, vol. 2, p. 94–95)

The patience of Charlsie is a humbling lesson to all who know her, and the source of her wisdom is a gift offered freely to everyone. Perhaps you know someone with this kind of patience and faith. Yes, the world shall mock, and we shall suffer. Our natural tendency is to dwell on our feelings—our fears, our doubts, our perceived injustices, and our impatience. If, however, we keep our eyes on God's promises and the eternal view, we realize that what we suffer here and now amounts to nothing but fleeting shadows. We live life in confidence in the peace that passes understanding. We rely on Jesus' precious promise to give us the joy that no one can take away from us.

Cherishing the Word

1. What is the foundation of a Christian's patience?

2. In what ways is complaining an obstacle to faith?

3. According to Luther, what is the remedy for those times when our faith seems to go "dry"?

> Heed the Word and say, Now then! Let's be patient for a little while yet; the Lord will be gracious to us and allow Himself again to be seen.... That precious promise is the heart of this Gospel lesson, truly good news for us Christians, so that we may keep on growing in faith. It is finally faith alone that can bring us the comfort, the patience, and the hope we need for all of life's great trials and tribulations. (Third Sunday after Easter, vol. 2, p. 95)

• What words can I say to myself when I feel persecuted by others for my faith?

• How might I take instruction and comfort in the way that Jesus spoke to His disciples in the Scripture reading?

• What are some of the things I complain about? What strategies will I use to stop my complaining and instead find God's peace and joy?

• What insights or blessings would I like to share with others?

> Do you not know? Have you not heard?
> The Lord is the everlasting God,
>   the creator of the end of the earth...
> Even youths grow tired and weary,
>   and young men stumble and fall;
> but those who hope in the LORD
>   will renew their strength.
> They will soar on wings like eagles;
>   they will run and not grow weary,
> they will walk and not be faint. (Isaiah 40:28–31)

Reflections

6

CHERISH THE PREACHED WORD OF GOD

We listen to and treasure the Word of God.

Jesus spoke to them again in parables, saying, "The kingdom of heaven is like a king who prepared a wedding banquet for his son. He sent his servants to those who had been invited to the banquet to tell them to come, but they refused to come.

"Then he sent some more servants, and said, 'Tell those who have been invited that I have prepared my dinner: My oxen and fattened cattle have been butchered, and everything is ready. Come to the wedding banquet.'

"But they paid no attention and went off—one to his field, another to his business. The rest seized his servants, mistreated them and killed them. The king was enraged. He sent his army and destroyed those murderers and burned their city.

"Then he said to his servants, 'The wedding banquet is ready, but those I invited did not deserve to come. Go to the street corners and invite to the banquet anyone you find.' So the servants went out into the streets and gathered all the people they could find, both good and bad, and the wedding hall was filled with guests.

"But when the king came into see the guests, he noticed a man there who was not wearing wedding clothes. 'Friend,' he asked, 'how did you get in here without wedding clothes?' The man was speechless.

"Then the king told the attendants, 'Tie him hand and foot, and throw him outside, into the darkness, where there will be weeping and gnashing of teeth.'

"For many are invited, but few are chosen." (Matthew 22:1–14)

As a first-time visitor to a mainline suburban church, I had taken a seat for the Sunday morning service. The hymns had been sung, the prayers said, the offering taken, and the creed recited. Now the spotlight illuminated the pulpit, and the pastor was delivering the day's sermon. After a few minutes I found that I liked the preacher's style of delivery. I could feel his sincerity and appreciate the biblical substance of his message.

Soon, however, I began to sense that something was wrong. I found that I was distracted again and again by things going on around me. Repeatedly I tried to concentrate on the pastor's words, but eventually my attention was drawn away. Finally despairing of keeping my focus, I turned my full attention to the scene around me.

At once I was struck by the level of noise and commotion in and among the pews. In the pew directly ahead, a boy crumpled his bulletin and repeatedly kicked the hymnal rack with his hard shoes, while his mother whispered to a friend at her side. Farther forward I saw a pew full of an extended family—obviously old-timers and pillars of the church—having a slightly muted social time regardless of their surroundings. To the right a few teenagers slipped out for their third trip to the restrooms. To the left an elderly man was dozing off, filling the air with the raspy refrains of his heavy nasal breathing.

Annoyed by the people around me, I tried to imagine how Martin Luther himself would have handled such disrespect from his congregation. I recalled the sermon on the king's wedding feast, where Pastor Luther admonished his congregation to give God's Word the respect and reverence it deserves. In his typical direct and unflinching manner, Luther warned against the kind of religious security that despises the preaching of the Word. Because the preached Gospel is the very Word of God, the complacent habit of neglecting or ignoring the sermon is seen as nothing less than the most grievous of sins! In his sermon on the parable of the wedding banquet, Luther put it this way:

> There is a great deal about us that is contrary to our Lord God and justly displeases Him—things like anger, impatience, greed, belly-serving, sexual voyeurism, evil lusts, fornication, hatred, and other vices which are nothing other than abominable mortal sins—rampant everywhere in the world. But such sins are nothing compared to the terrible disdain of the divine Word. Disdain that is so deep and so pervasive, that in truth, greed, stealing, adultery, whoremongering, and so forth, cannot even compare; yes, indeed, these sins would be as nothing if people would only love and esteem God's Word. However, sad to say, the opposite is the case and, as a result, the whole world is inundated by such sins. (Twentieth Sunday after Trinity, vol. 3, pp. 93–94)

Never one to let nominal Christians sit comfortably in their pews imagining they are doing God a great favor by their mere presence, Luther thunders against those who nod off to sleep, those who whisper and talk, and those who daydream idly during the sermon. He adds, "Truly, I am shocked to see how people in the church, on the right and on the left, yawn away, so that out of a great throng there are hardly ten or twelve who are actually present in order to learn something from the preaching" (94). This observation comes from an era when sermons regularly lasted well over an hour; how much less would Luther excuse us whose sermons tend to be merely a few minutes long?

The issue is not a trivial one, says Luther, and the very fact that people no longer consider it important is a sign of sin within the church. Luther laments:

> But worse still is the fact that this disregard of God's Word is now so commonplace that this truly terrible, hellish, devilish sin is not even regarded as being sin at all, like other sins. Everyone simply dismisses it as a trifling matter that people fail to listen diligently to preaching; yes, the majority hold that opinion, believing that wine and beer taste just as good when listening to preaching of the Word as at any other time. Nobody is bothered by this, much less does anyone make it a matter of conscience for having such little regard for the beloved Word. This does not happen in connection with other sins, like murder, adultery, and robbery; for with them there is remorse, if not sooner then later, because the heart is horrified and wishes it would never have been. But, for inattention to God's Word, yes, for despising and ridiculing it, for this no one has conscience scruples. (Twentieth Sunday after Trinity, vol. 3, p. 94)

Satan's greatest victories do not lie in getting unbelievers to heap vice upon vice, but in lulling believers into taking God's Word lightly.

Citing John 3:19 in this regard, Luther asserts that following this path of disregarding God's Word leads to destruction. God also turns them over to errors and the folly of self-righteousness. But worst of all, says Luther, God will say to us, "Since you do not want to listen to me when I speak, I shall no longer listen" to you. Luther adds a real jolt here by quoting Proverbs 1:24–33. Read it—if you have any sense, it'll make you shiver. As God reveals Himself to us in His Word through preaching, our seemingly harmless whisperings and reveries during the sermon become an offense to God.

What can we do? As usual, Luther is clear and direct on this point. "We must, therefore, learn to guard against this sin, esteem God's Word highly, and hearken to it diligently and gladly" (96). In other words, to listen carefully to God's Word for a few minutes each week is hardly asking too much, when we consider that this Word is the means to our eternal salvation and our lifeline to the loving Creator. Luther's warning is clear that believers will experience grief unless we are diligent in respecting and listening to God's Word while we still have it freely available to us.

In the church where I visited, the congregation stood and somewhat mechanically sang the closing hymn, "More About Jesus Would I Know" after the sermon. My irritation about the distractions had tempted me to blame the others and resent their inattention, rudeness, and disrespect. But upon reflection I had to admit that I allowed myself to be distracted as well, and I too ended by eclipsing God's Word with my own thoughts and feelings. So, it seems that Luther's homily on the king's banquet is not only for the others in the congregation; it is for me as well.

> Each Christian, therefore, should diligently devote himself to such service and think: Since my Lord and God so wants me to hear His Word and regards this service so highly that he readily accepts it as a service pleasing to Him, I shall gladly render it, proclaim, hear, read, and learn His Word.... For to serve such a great Lord, as God is, is a wonderful thing. All of us, therefore, ought be ready to say, Dear God, daily you shower countless kindnesses on me; therefore, since You want me to give ear to Your Word, I shall in service to you and to your glory diligently and earnestly do so and be careful not to despise it. (Twentieth Sunday after Trinity, vol. 3, pp. 96–97)

I remember God's mercy in Christ—mercy to *me*. For all my failures, Christ is ready to forgive, to restore, to strengthen. His "countless kindnesses" in my life only draw me to appreciate the Gospel in all its grace and power. What a wonderful gift—a treasure to cherish forever.

Cherishing the Word

1. Explain how the parable of the king's wedding feast relates to Luther's comments on the preaching of the Word.

2. We live in a society that spends a great deal of its resources on entertainment. How might this "entertainment mentality" affect our attitudes toward the preached Word?

3. Is inattention to the sermon really the great sin that Luther says it is? Why or why not? What does the Bible say concerning this issue?

> Let us, therefore... gladly and diligently hear the Word and in all good faith regard those who invite to the wedding feast as dear and precious, for the sake of the Lord who sends them out. Then the Lord will be with us in every need, help and protect us, and finally give us eternal life for the sake of His Son, our loving bridegroom, Christ the Lord. (Twentieth Sunday after Trinity, vol. 3, p. 99)

• Do I cherish God's Word? How do I demonstrate that I care about his Word?

• What do I appreciate most about my congregation's worship?

• In what ways can I learn more about God's Word?

• What insights or blessings would I like to share with others?

> I have hidden Your word in my heart
>   that I might not sin against You.
> Praise be to You, O Lord; teach me Your decrees.
> With my lips I recount all the laws
>   that come from Your mouth.
> I rejoice in following Your statutes
>   as one rejoices in great riches.
> I meditate on Your precepts and consider Your ways.
> I delight in Your decrees;
>   I will not neglect Your word. (Psalm 119:11–16)

Reflections

7

REAL FAITH LEADS TO JOY

*We experience anew the joy that comes
from the marvelous gift of the Christ child.*

The child's father and mother marveled at what was
said about Him. Then Simeon blessed them and said to
Mary, His mother: "This child is destined to cause the
falling and rising of many in Israel, and to be a sign
that will be spoken against, so that the thoughts of
many hearts will be revealed. And a sword will pierce
your own soul too."

There was also a prophetess, Anna, the daughter of
Phanuel, of the tribe of Asher. She was very old; she had
lived with her husband seven years after her marriage,
and then was a widow until she was eighty-four. She
never left the temple but worshiped night and day, fasting and praying. Coming up to them at that very
moment, she gave thanks to God and spoke about the
child to all who were looking forward to the redemption of Jerusalem.

When Joseph and Mary had done everything required
by the Law of the Lord, they returned to Galilee to their
own town of Nazareth. And the child grew and became
strong; He was filled with wisdom, and the grace of God
was upon Him. (Luke 2:33–40)

My wife Lynn absolutely and thoroughly adores all babies. No matter what the circumstances or what her previous mood, the mere sight of a new baby always brings a light of pure joy into her face. It's just something inside her, something spontaneous and profound that intrinsically delights her to the depths of her soul.

Sometimes she makes me think of the prophetess Anna, who came upon Mary and Joseph carrying the infant Jesus in the temple courtyard. I like to imagine Anna's face lighting up with that same joy at the sight of baby Jesus, and then to think of that multiplied delight at the knowledge of who that special baby really was.

Martin Luther's homily on the aged Simeon and the prophetess Anna is based on the account of their blessing the baby Jesus at the temple in Jerusalem. Christians have ample cause to rejoice daily because of the great gift of this holy child to a world lost in darkness. Speaking of Simeon's blessing, Luther explains:

> He tells how that little child is a Saviour, the one whom God has prepared for all people and a light which would illuminate all the heathen. The child, he says, was not to be a small, limited light, as before when God shone His light only on the Jews, but a far-reaching, brilliant light which, like the sun, would illumine the whole world. (First Sunday after Christmas, vol. 1, p. 154)

The birth of Jesus means that salvation is not only for the Jews, but for everyone in the world. Luther emphasizes the great importance of these testimonies by Simeon and Anna, as they assert that Jesus is indeed the fulfillment of the Old Testament prophecies of the coming Messiah.

> The patriarch Simeon steps up, even though by virtue of age he can scarcely see his way, and with penetrating clarity of discernment recognizes and praises this child as the Saviour and Light of the World. All emperors, kings, and sovereigns are mere darkness, but this child is the Light of the World. All the world is subjugated

under death and damnation, but through this child the world will obtain salvation. This child, in short, is the one whom the prophets foretold. (First Sunday after Christmas, vol. 1, pp. 154–55)

If we can fully fathom what this Christ child means for us, we cannot help being overcome by joy.

In other sermons Luther speaks of the hardships and persecutions that we can expect to result from our faith. In this homily, though, he speaks of the deeper relationship between faith and joy. In this regard he says:

That is the unique nature of faith, that the firmer one believes, the more one marvels and the happier one is. In contrast, when faith is absent, there is neither joy nor enthusiasm. Thus, if this were a certainty in my heart and I believed without doubt that this child, born of the Virgin Mary, is my brother, yes, my flesh and blood, and that His righteousness is my righteousness...I say, if I were to believe this with all my heart, then I would so marvel and be so overjoyed that I could not think enough about this infant child. (First Sunday after Christmas, vol. 1, p. 156)

What Jesus has done for us is truly amazing, and yet we have so hardened our hearts that we go about our lives and even our worship in a state of dour, sour-faced seriousness.

Luther asks where we can find Christians whose joy in their salvation, whose victory over sin and death, and whose awe and gratitude to Christ shine in their faces. He adds:

We can all repeat the words, but whether we truly believe is soon evident, because there is no joy, no amazement, no change in us. If one wishes to call that faith, surely it is cold, half-dead faith.... For a Christian is a happy, confident, redeemed person who is sidetracked neither by the devil nor by any trouble. For he knows that through Christ he is master over all this. (First Sunday after Christmas, vol. 1, p. 157)

In other words, faith is a marvelous victory and Christians know how to enjoy the fruits of victory.

Is Luther advocating a kind of self-righteous pride? Is he suggesting that Christians should feel smug and superior to those who are lost in their unbelief? Is he calling us to an irresponsible pursuit of luxuries and good times? He is certainly not. Christians, he explains, "do not vaunt themselves by virtue of what they are, but rather they exult over that which has been given them by grace" (157). All of the glory belongs to God and Luther reminds us that, despite our many troubles, the daily impulse of our souls ought to be gratefulness, humility, and joy.

Just as the very sight of a newborn baby never fails to bring great joy to my wife Lynn, so the very thought of the newborn Savior ought to bring even greater joy and gratitude to our souls. Our rejoicing over the Christ child should not be limited to once a year at the Christmas season, but our entire lives can reflect our spontaneous joy for the miraculous gift of the child-Savior, Jesus Christ. Luther says that if we daily contemplate the baby Jesus, our hearts will indeed join with the angels in their joyful chorus: Glory to God in the highest!

FROM HEAVEN ABOVE TO EARTH I COME

From heav'n above to earth I come
  To bring good news to ev'ryone!
Glad tidings of great joy I bring
  To all the world and gladly sing:

To you this night is born a child
  Of Mary, chosen virgin mild;
This newborn child of lowly birth
  Shall be the joy of all the earth.

This is the Christ, God's Son, most high,
  Who hears your sad and bitter cry;
He will Himself your Savior be
  And from all sin will set you free.

Look, look, dear friends, look over there!
  What lies within that manger bare?
Who is that lovely little one?
  The baby Jesus, God's dear Son.

—Martin Luther (1534/5)

Cherishing the Word

1. Why are the blessings uttered by Simeon and Anna so vitally important?

2. Why does Luther say that a faith without joy is a "cold, half-dead" faith?

3. In what ways is Christian joy fundamentally opposed to both pridefulness and irresponsible hedonism?

> The gospel should instill such amazement in us that we too would exult and proudly assert: I have been baptized in Christ; there is not doubt, that through the Lord Jesus, I become a lord and can overcome death and sin, and heaven and all creation must serve my best interests. (First Sunday after Christmas, vol. 1, p. 156)

• Do I really think of the Christ child as a precious gift from God to me? Am I amazed and joyful over His incarnation and birth?

• What are some specific ways that I can "soften" my heart and prepare myself more fully to receive the joy that faith brings?

• My prayer of praise expressing wonder, gratitude and joy over the gift of the Christ child.

• What insights or blessings would I like to share with others?

> Praise be to the God and Father of our Lord Jesus Christ!" In His great mercy He has given us new birth into a living hope through the resurrection of Jesus Christ from the dead, and into an inheritance that can never perish, spoil or fade—kept in heaven for you, who through faith are shielded by God's power until the coming of the salvation that is ready to be revealed in the last time. (1 Peter 1:3–5)

Reflections

WELCOME TO EARTH, O NOBLE GUEST

Welcome to earth, O noble Guest,
　　Through whom this sinful world is blest!
You turned not from our needs away!
　　How can our thanks such love repay?

O Lord, You have created all!
　　How did You come to be so small
To sweetly sleep in manger bed
　　Where lowing cattle lately fed?

Were earth a thousand times as fair
　　And set with gold and jewels rare,
Still such a cradle would not do
　　To rock a prince as great as You.

O dearest Jesus, holy Child,
　　Prepare a bed, soft, undefiled,
A holy shrine, within my heart,
　　That You and I need never part.

—Martin Luther (1534/5)

8

Merciful, as God Is Merciful

As we live in Christ, we imitate God's mercy.

"Be merciful, just as your Father is merciful.

"Do not judge, and you will not be judged. Do not condemn, and you will not be condemned. Forgive, and you will be forgiven. Give, and it will be given to you. A good measure, pressed down, shaken together and running over, will be poured into your lap. For with the measure you use, it will be measured to you."

He also told them this parable: "Can a blind man lead a blind man? Will they not both fall into a pit? A student is not above his teacher, but everyone who is fully trained will be like his teacher."

"Why do you look at the speck of sawdust in your brother's eye and pay no attention to the plank in your own eye? How can you say to your brother, 'Brother, let me take the speck out of your eye, when you yourself fail to see the plank in your own eye? You hypocrite, first take the plank out of your eye, and then you will see clearly to remove the speck from your brother's eye." (Luke 6:36–42)

Excuse me for saying this," said my nonbelieving friend, "but the most rigid and unforgiving people I know are people who call themselves Christians." These words are always hard for me to hear, but there are times that I find myself very close to agreeing. I think we all know professing Christians who would be among the last we would call *merciful* people.

This issue is complicated, however, by the fact that Christians are called to meet a moral standard—God's standard—and may genuinely struggle to hold the line in their personal lives against the unrelenting onslaught of immoral and amoral values in our contemporary world. What may look like rigidity or self-righteous condemnation to a free-floating relativist is often a courageous and faithful act of insistence upon what is good and right in a given situation.

On the other hand, honesty compels me to admit that unmerciful attitudes are far too numerous among those who frequent the churches. Even worse, I must confess the many times that I myself have been unmerciful—perhaps in the name of upholding and defending Christian morality. The ugly truth is that I and others like me are capable of being downright judgmental and callous in our moral responses to the people around us. Luther's message in this homily is that we are without excuse; when we are unmerciful we "fall short of the glory of God" (Romans 3:23).

Without compromising a millimeter on God's holiness and justice, Martin Luther boldly preaches God's mercy as well. In fact, the point of this homily on Luke 6:36–42 is to say that mercy occupies the center of the Gospel, and to speak of faith and morals devoid of mercy is utter folly. Jesus Christ is our visual demonstration of God's mercy to us, and our mercy to others is a demonstration of our faith in God and our discipleship in Christ.

To those who would accuse Christians of adulating faith at the expense of love and good works, Luther replies clearly, saying that a faith which does not manifest itself in works of love toward others is no faith at all! Yes, this is the same Luther who ignited the Reformation by insisting that our salvation is based on faith alone and that a mountain of good deeds cannot achieve our salvation or righteousness. How then can he now say that works of love are a proof of our faith?

From the gospel lesson, Luther paraphrases Jesus' sermon:

Christ here wants to ward off such pretense and teach us to truly believe. For that reason He doesn't introduce a strange and unfamiliar example for us but one involving our heavenly Father and our own experience in His dealing with us. In gist He is saying, Your faith is genuine when you do unto your neighbor as your Father in heaven has done to you...

Because of your sins you were all under God's judgement and condemnation. And what did your Father in heaven then do? Is it not true that He neither wanted to judge nor condemn you, but forgave you all your sins, suspended His judgement, and accepted you in grace? For that you should be grateful and do to your neighbor as your Father has done to you: be merciful, judge not, neither condemn, but forgive and be gracious as your Father in heaven has forgiven and been gracious to you. (Fourth Sunday after Trinity, vol. 2, pp. 276–77)

The same point is made in Matthew 18:21–35 in the parable of the unmerciful servant. If we really believe in God, we will be merciful to others as God is merciful to us. However, false Christians do not like to hear this part of the sermon, says Luther. They like to hear the gospel message about God's forgiveness, but they would rather not hear that God, in mercy, has called them to live in His grace, forgiving others and serving all people. In this regard Luther says, "They enjoy sermons about grace and forgiveness of sins.... Such a sermon, I say, the pseudo-Christians like to hear; but that they, in turn, should show mercy, love, compassion, friendliness, and every kindness, with that they will have nothing to do" (278). Luther calls such people false Christians precisely because their lack of compassion reveals that their faith is not real.

Here Luther reveals one of the most pervasive problems in the church today: the eclipse of "good old-fashioned" mercy by other practices and trappings of religion. This theme also runs through the famous "love chapter," 1 Corinthians 13. No matter how pious, how fervent, how "spiritual," how popular, how satisfying, faith remains worthless if we do not show mercy to the people whom God places near us in our daily lives.

Luther concludes, "That's why this gospel presses for the fruits of faith, showing that if fruit does not follow faith, it is a sign that our faith is not genuine" (278).

Here is an important insight indeed, for it corrects an error that is commonly heard in discussions of Luther's doctrine. Far from saying that good works are worthless, Luther insists that true faith necessarily produces the fruit of good deeds. "Clearly," he concludes, "none may boast of his faith unless it be proved with good fruit and deed" (280). In other words, charity and compassion are not "extras" that Christians can do as a favor to God; they are essential to the living of our faith. Without such works of love, we have no faith of which to speak.

If our faith is only talk, says Luther, God will withdraw its benefits from us. Paraphrasing what God says to "counterfeit Christians," Luther continues:

> You wicked Christian, I have given you my Word, baptism, the Lord's Supper, eternal life and salvation, a good conscience and joy, also your very body and life, and every material possession; and you should have dealt with your fellowman in like manner.... That should have been the verifying token by which you could have known whether you truly believed, or not.... You have not been merciful.... Very well, I will withdraw my grace and mercy; I will take back my forgiveness, eternal life, and the salvation that I granted you. I will not forgive you, even as you have not forgiven your fellowman. (Fourth Sunday after Trinity, vol. 2, p. 277)

Our lack of mercy and compassion is much more serious than merely a bad habit. It is a sign that we have not truly believed God and received His grace.

For our many failures, though, Luther has a word of comfort in Christ. Our Lord Jesus has demonstrated His mercy to us in His sacrificial life, death, and resurrection. Forgiveness radiates from the cross to every part of our life, including our obstinate pride. The Savior's goodness flows over into our lives and through His Spirit He works to draw us closer to His character. God is conforming us "to the likeness of His Son" (Romans 8:29) and He gives us His strength for our journey.

> As I stood alone before God, he measured me graciously. If he were here to assess us according to our deserts, we would deserve wrath, disquiet, and all kinds of misery. We would deserve to have the earth swallow us up as soon as we were born, not to mention the fact that through our entire life we conducted ourselves in such an evil way that we rightly deserved death and hell. But what does God do? He throws out everything that we deserve: anger, disgrace, judgment, death, and hell, and gives us heaven, grace, and freedom from the Law's accusation and our bad conscience. He throws out all deficiencies and guilt, and grants all good things. (Fourth Sunday after Trinity, vol. 2, p. 280)

Cherishing the Word

1. When Luther says we are saved by "faith alone," does he mean that works of love are unimportant to our faith?

2. What, according to Luther, will God do if we fail to show compassion to others?

3. What is the point of the parable of the unmerciful servant from Matthew 18:21–35?

> This is a wonderful sermon, for we see that God places an even greater emphasis on services to one's fellow-man than service to Him. For He, on His part, forgives all sins and does not avenge Himself for what we have done wrong to Him…. Now, because we received such measure from God, he says to us, Remember, measure in the same way with other people. (Fourth Sunday after Trinity, vol. 2, p. 281)

• Am I merciful as God is merciful? Do people know me as a compassionate person? What about people whom I don't know? What do they see in how I act toward them?

• When I take an honest look at the visible fruit of my faith, what are my strong areas? My weak areas? How can I improve in these matters?

• My prayer—confession, petition, or praise—to God on this matter of compassion and mercy.

• What insights or blessings would I like to share with others?

> Dear friends, since God so loved us, we also ought to love one another. No one has ever seen God; but if we love one another, God lives in us and His love is made complete in us.
>
> We know that we live in Him and He in us, because He has given us of His Spirit. And we have seen and testify that the Father has sent His Son to be the Savior of the world. If anyone acknowledges that Jesus is the Son of God, God lives in him and he in God. And so we know and rely on the love God has for us. (1 John 4:11–16)

Reflections

9

DEALING WITH TEMPTATIONS

*In the grace and strength of Christ,
we find help in our temptations.*

Then Jesus was led by the Spirit into the desert to be tempted by the devil. After fasting forty days and forty nights, He was hungry. The tempter came to Him and said, "If you are the Son of God tell these stones to become bread."

Jesus answered, "It is written: 'Man does not live on bread alone, but on every word that comes from the mouth of God.'

Then the devil took Him to the holy city and had Him stand on the highest point of the temple. "If you are the Son of God," he said, "throw yourself down. For it is written:

"'He will command his angels concerning you, and they will lift you up in their hands,so that you will not strike your foot against a stone.'"

Jesus answered him, "It is also written: 'Do not put the Lord your God to the test.'"

Again, the devil took Him to a very high mountain and showed Him all the kingdoms of the world and their splendor. "All this I will give you," He said, "If you will bow down and worship me."

Jesus said to him, "Away from me, Satan! For it is written: 'Worship the Lord your God, and serve Him only.'"

Then the devil left Him, and angels came and attended Him. (Matthew 4:1–11)

Martin Luther's sermon for the First Sunday in Lent examines Jesus' three temptations in the wilderness. In the same ways that Satan tempted Jesus, so does Satan assault us Christians as well. On this subject Luther says:

All Christians face such attack, for the adversary never relents but continues to try to wrench us away from Christ and our baptism, by means of hunger or persecution, by worldly fame and wealth, or by heresy or false interpretation of Scripture, so that we give way to despair and vain glory. If such tricks fail, the devil tries to get us by the throat and strangle us to death. (First Sunday in Lent, vol. 1, p. 313)

There is much to consider here, but for me one thought is essential. Luther clearly unmasks Satan's ultimate goals: that we be conquered through our despair or through our pride and finally destroyed. In other words, all of our temptations are carefully and diabolically designed to enslave us and kill us.

If you are anything like me, you may have noticed an irritating propensity in yourself to live your life in cycles. There are times when I feel good, right, powerful, and effective. Next thing I know I'm feeling rather smug about it all, not realizing that I've already been tripped up by my pride. Then, of course, pride produces the inevitable fall, sending me along the pathway of frustration, disappointment, self-recrimination, and onto the road to despair.

But aren't despair and pride something close to opposites? How can they both serve to ensnare and bind us? Luther indicates here that they are not opposites at all; that they are the two sides of the same counterfeit coin. The real opposite to both is the hope and humility that is native to Christian faith. So, Satan is perfectly happy to keep me flopping back and forth between despair and pride, as long as I never find my solid footing on the path of faith between them. Luther says that we can learn to overcome the adversary through true faith in God and His Word.

Jesus' first temptation—to turn the stones into bread— is not so much concerned with a miracle, but it really amounts to a pernicious suggestion that God the Father does not care about Jesus. Speaking of Jesus, Luther explains:

> He knows very well what the devil is after and that he is not particularly interested in Jesus performing a miracle. Rather, as we see from Christ's reply, Satan wanted very much to rob Him of faith and reliance on God's loving kindness and to prompt the thought in His heart, God has forgotten You; He's indifferent to Your needs; He's willing to let You die of hunger, begrudging you even a piece of bread.... So, the devil's prompting is this: Your only concern is for bread; forget about God's Word; bread is what You need. (First Sunday in Lent, vol. 1, pp. 314–15)

From this incident, says Luther, we should learn to distinguish between the two kinds of bread. There is the temporal kind of bread that nourishes the body but allows that everlasting hunger to return. Then there is the bread of God's Word, the kind of nourishment that bestows eternal life. Clearly we ought to value God's Word much more highly than we value any temporal things.

In the second temptation Satan suggests that Jesus throw Himself down from a high tower, for if He is the Son of God the angels will surely prevent any harm coming to Him. Thus, having failed in his first approach, Satan attempts the opposite tactic. Luther explains:

> For if the devil cannot cause us to despair of God's benevolence, he brazenly tries next to see if he can make us proud and reckless enough to rely on our own

righteousness. It as though the devil were saying Christ,
If you want to argue with me from the Word of God,
hold on! I am able to do that also.... So jump off, and
let's see whether You believe that promise of God. (First
Sunday in Lent, vol. 1, p. 316)

Notice that here Satan even quotes Scriptures in his
attempt to deceive Jesus into performing an unnecessary miracle. Luther warns us Christians against manipulating the Word
of God in order to support our own religious agendas. Luther
says that we must not be "prompted merely by our own ideas of
religion, but in faithful conformity and obedience to the Word
of God in all that we do" (314).

The third temptation of Jesus also involves setting human
traditions and doctrines above the Word of God. Luther says:

It is a vile temptation by which Satan impudently offers
temporal honor and power, trying to lead us into idola-
try contrary to the Word of God. It helps that outward,
human righteousness has such a tremendous appeal to
reason and glitters far more enchantingly than does
obedience to God's Word, obedience to father and
mother, and doing what God commands him to do.
(First Sunday in Lent, vol. 1, p. 318)

This temptation is the urge toward self-made ideas of
righteousness and toward religion whose real function is to
make people feel important and powerful. Long-standing
church members are particularly vulnerable to this temptation,
as Satan uses leadership positions in the church to appeal to the
human ego. Essentially, whenever we feel like "big-shots," the
Tempter has won.

Hence, as Christians we can expect that Satan will continue to insinuate into our minds these three temptations: the
despairing thought that God doesn't care about us; the prideful
urge toward showy spirituality; and the perennial craving for
wealth, power, and fame. However, says Luther, these temptations can be overcome, first by listening carefully to the Word
of God, and second by earnestly praying "that God would let

his kingdom come among us, not lead us into temptation, but graciously deliver us from all evil" (313).

We do not endure and overcome alone, however. Jesus our brother suffers with us. The Lord who suffered for us, despising the shame of the cross, is God-Man, the Son of God who takes to Himself our weakness and sin. Baptized into His death and resurrection, we are enlisted in His service, marshaled, Luther writes, "into an army in confrontation with the devil" (313). We now follow Christ. We now walk in His ways. When we are tempted, we trust our Lord to be there. As Luther notes, "If the devil is assailing you through persecution, want, hunger, and affliction, suffer it and fast with Christ, since it is the Spirit who directs you, and do not let up on your trust in God's grace. In time the angels will wait on your table" (316).

In His grace and strength, we stand.

Cherishing the Word

1. What do each of Jesus' three temptations mean?

2. What is the significance of the fact that Satan quotes Scriptures during the second temptation?

3. According to Luther, what are the two best ways that we can overcome temptations?

> As long as we live, we can expect all three of these temptations. We must, therefore, gird ourselves well with God's Word, in order to protect and sustain ourselves. May Christ, our dear Lord, who himself overcame these temptations for our good, give us also the strength through Him to overcome and to be saved. (First Sunday in Lent, vol. 1, p. 320)

• How does Jesus' experience of intense temptation make me feel about my own times of temptation?

• When I find that I have given in to temptation, what do I generally do?

• Which of these three kinds of temptation is the most powerful in my life? How can I draw closer to Christ and overcome temptations?

• What insights or blessings would I like to share with others?

> Therefore, since we have a great high priest who has gone through the heavens, Jesus the Son of God, let us hold firmly to the faith we profess. For we do not have a high priest who is unable to sympathize with our weaknesses, but we have one who has been tempted in every way, just as we are—yet was without sin. Let us then approach the throne of grace with confidence, so that we may receive mercy and find grace to help us in our time of need. (Hebrews 4:14–16)

Reflections

A Mighty Fortress Is Our God

A mighty fortress is our God,
    A trusty shield and weapon;
He helps us free from ev'ry need
    That hath us now o'ertaken.
The old evil foe Now means deadly woe;
Deep guile and great might Are His dread arms in fight;
On earth is not His equal.

With might of ours can naught be done,
    Soon were our loss effected;
But for us fights the valiant One,
    Whom God Himself elected.
Ask ye, Who is this? Jesus Christ it is,
Of sabaoth Lord, And there's none other God;
He holds the field forever.

Though devils all the world should fill,
    All eager to devour us,
We tremble not, we fear no ill,
    They shall not overpow'r us.
This world's prince may still Scowl fierce as he will,
He can harm us none, He's judged; the deed is done;
One little word can fell him.

The Word they still shall let remain
    Nor any thanks have for it;
He's by our side upon the plain
    With His good gifts and Spirit.
And take they our life, Goods, fame, child, and wife,
Though these all be gone, Our vict'ry has been won;
The Kingdom ours remaineth.

—*Martin Luther (1520s)*

10
LET GOD BE GOD

*We appreciate God's gracious will
and recognize the folly of human efforts
to define, second-guess, or manipulate God.*

"For the kingdom of heaven is like a landowner who went out early in the morning to hire men to work in his vineyard. He agreed to pay them a denarius for the day and sent them into his vineyard.

"About the third hour he went out and saw others standing in the marketplace doing nothing. He told them, 'You also go and work in my vineyard, and I will pay you whatever is right. So they went.

"He went out again about the sixth hour and the ninth hour and did the same thing. About the eleventh hour he went out and found still others standing around. He asked them, 'Why have you been standing here all day long doing nothing?'

'Because no one has hired us,' they answered.

"He said to them, 'You also go and work in my vineyard.'

"When evening came, the owner of the vineyard said to his foreman, 'Call the workers and pay them their wages, beginning with the last ones hired and going on to the first.'

"The workers who were hired about the eleventh hour came and each received a denarius. So when those came who were hired first, they expected to receive more. But each one of them also received a denarius. Whey they received it, they began to grumble against the land-owner. 'These men who were hired last worked only one hour,' they said, 'and you have made them equal to us who have borne the burden of the work and the heat of the day.'

"But he answered one of them, 'Friend, I am not being unfair to you. Didn't you agree to work for a denarius? Take your pay and go. I want to give the man who was hired last the same as I gave you. Don't I have the right to do what I want with my own money? Or are you envious because I am generous?'

"So the last will be first, and the first will be last." (Matthew 20:1–16)

The first time I saw the phrase, "Let God be God," I was reading one of those formidable tomes by Karl Barth on Christian theology. Frankly the statement puzzled me. If God is truly omnipotent, then He doesn't need us mere mortals to "let" Him do anything. "Let God Be God" seems to give us too much power in the relationship. I would discover later that my initial perplexity came from my misunderstanding of what Barth had in mind, as I came to realize that his meaning was actually the same as what both Luther and Calvin meant by the otherness and sovereignty of God. The phrase might have expressed the idea more truly if it had said, "Realize that God is God."

The issue here is not merely the mincing of words; it is important and particularly relevant for our times. People—even Christians who should know better—forget what it means that God is *God*. There is a continual and progressive blurring of the distinct boundaries between the Creator and the creation, a gradual eroding of the truth that God is wholly other than humankind and, in Himself, far beyond our human understanding. The instances of eroding and blurring are subtle and many, and thus all the more destructive.

Among the major themes in the Bible from beginning to end is the enduring propensity of human beings to substitute their own egos, standards, values, and ideas for those of God. The lion's share of the "liberal theologies" of the past two centuries have sought to reconfigure the relationship between God and His creatures in such ways as to make God, in effect, the dependent variable. Today we find "Christian" writers trying to define God as everything from the subconscious mind to whatever might be "re-imagined" by the participants at a conference. As C. S. Lewis observed, Christians have always seemed intent on "taming" God, trying to make God conform to our personal views and lifestyles. Luther reminds us, however, that the almighty, living God will not be tamed nor pigeonholed, no matter what we may imagine.

In this sermon Martin Luther addresses the difficult parable of the workmen and their wages. Recalling that at the end of the day the employer paid all of the workers the same amount—no matter how many hours each had worked—Luther observes that such an arrangement offends our ideas of what is right and just in the relationship between workers and their employer. But then he adds, *that* is the very point of the parable. Jesus intentionally told a story in which the actions of the employer seem unfair to us.

As Luther explains, the parable is really about God, the point is that God can do whatever He pleases. Luther says:

> The Lord told the parable in this fashion so as to distinguish clearly between His kingdom and the worldly realm, and thus to remind us that His kingdom operates with principles different from the standards of the world. On the worldly scene there can be no equality simply because people themselves are so diverse. That's

why, as a general rule, he who has labored more, also receives more pay.... Such disparity exists of necessity in the worldly realm. In Christ's kingdom, however, there should be no such difference. All are to be equal, one the same as the other; each to have and be "worth" as much as the next one. (Septuagesima Sunday, vol. 1, p. 279)

We cannot apply our notions of justice to God's actions, for our ideas are so vastly different from those of God.

In a variety of applications of the parable Luther discusses the feelings of some people when they hear and understand the implications of equality in the kingdom of God. Though they want to be regarded as superior, they become "mad and furious" when their privileged status and positions are taken away. Likewise, lifelong Christians may resent the thought of a person living the life of a hellion, only to be saved and gain eternal life during the last moments before his or her death.

Though our human reason rebels and says that such things do not seem fair, Luther says we must let God be God, regardless of what we think or feel. We have absolutely no right to grumble. For whether we have labored long in our faith or are new Christians, we are all equal before God. God extends His grace to all people equally. Those who are saved, by His mercy, enter into a community of peers, a fellowship of saints. As if to share this wonderful truth in clear and powerful language, Luther strings gem after gem in his sermon:

In Christ's kingdom ... all are equal! None has a different baptism, gospel, faith, sacrament, or a different Christ or God. Together they all go to church; servant, townsman, farmer all hear the same Word as the lord, prince, and nobleman hear. The baptism I have is the same one that any little maid receives; the faith Peter and Paul had is the same faith Magdalene and the thief on the cross had; as Christians you and I also have it. (Septuagesima Sunday, vol. 1, p. 280)

And so let the world operate with its inequality as best it can. We will continue to take comfort in the fact—our station being high or low—that we all have one Christ, one baptism, one Gospel, one Spirit. No one has a better gospel, a better baptism, a different or better Christ, or a different or better heaven—we are all equal! (Septuagesima Sunday, vol. 1, p. 280)

What we say is this: In Christ's kingdom all are equal; God deals with all of us not on the basis of merit but solely and alone according to grace and mercy—for the sake of His Son Christ Jesus. (Septuagesima Sunday, vol. 1, p. 282)

In His kingdom we are all to be equal, since we all have one and the same God, Christ, Holy Spirit, gospel, Holy Sacrament and faith. On account of such equality, each one of us is as good, pious, and holy as the next person. (Septuagesima Sunday, vol. 1, p. 283)

Though we cannot fully understand the justice—or the mercy—of God, we can begin to understand some of the reason in this parable. Luther says that it is as if God had said, "No one has ever succeeded in earning the kingdom of heaven—salvation from death and sin—and because of that I am not under obligation to anyone; always the kingdom comes by grace to whomsoever I will" (284).

Here again, then, is Luther's point about "grace alone." Not one of us has earned a single thing from God. Our salvation is an unmerited gift from God and the only appropriate responses are wonder and gratitude, not resentment and grumbling.

The more profound issue, however, is the relationship between us creatures and our Holy Creator. To be God means to possess power, knowledge, wisdom, goodness, justice, and love far beyond the reaches of human comprehension. What utter folly and audacity it is when we presume to question God's judgments and grumble against His ways. In this we become like the grumbling workmen in the parable. Instead, we remember the words of Psalm 46:10, "Be still, and know that I am God."

God is our Savior in Christ. His salvation, a gift to all, brings us joy.

Cherishing the Word

1. In what specific ways are we in the church always especially susceptible to the idea that we can earn or deserve God's favor?

2. Why is it not legitimate for a Christian to grumble about life being unfair?

3. How can we respond to the question, "How could a loving God let such a terrible thing happen to an innocent victim?"

> Knowing that in Christ's kingdom there is no inequality, we have courage and comfort, and in Christian "pride" we go forward to do what needs to be done. In this way everyone can go about his daily work in a joyful and godly manner. A Christian can truly say, I have no reason to grumble about my station in life; it is a good and precious one, even though it be unimportant and boring. It may not be a princely position but it is a Christian one; what more could I have or desire? (Septuagesima Sunday, vol. 1, p. 281)

• What are some of the ways I have tried to fit God into a mold of my own making?

• Do I sometimes become discontent and grumble against the actions (or apparent inaction) of God? What useful counsel can I find in today's lesson?

• What specific things can I do to keep myself always mindful of the gracious will of God?

• What insights or blessings would I like to share with others?

> What then shall we say? Is God unjust? Not at all!
> For He says to Moses,
> "I will have mercy on whom I have mercy,
> and I will have compassion on whom
>   I have compassion."
> It does not, therefore, depend on man's desire or effort,
> but on God's mercy. (Romans 9:14–16)

Reflections

11

COUNTERFEIT CHRISTIANS

*By God's grace, we look beyond
our human shortcomings in the church
and persevere in doing the work of God.*

Jesus told them another parable: "The kingdom of heaven is like a man who sowed good seed in his field. But while everyone was sleeping, his enemy came and sowed weeds among the wheat, and went away. When the wheat sprouted and formed heads, then the weeds also appeared.

The owner's servants came to him and said, 'Sir didn't you sow good seed in your field? Where then did the weeds come from?

'An enemy did this,' he replied.

The servants asked him, 'Do you want us to go and pull them up?'

'No,' he answered, 'because while you are pulling the weeds, you may root up the wheat with them. Let both grow together until the harvest. At that time I will tell the harvester: first collect the weeds and tie them in bundles to be burned; then gather the wheat and bring it into my barn.' (Matthew 13:24–30)

I am about to make another confession. My confession is that I have a much more difficult time in dealing with certain people in the church than I do with the other people in my life. Why is this so? Perhaps it results partly from the higher expectations I have of Christians. After all, we do have a common faith, we have clear biblical standards for living, and we know that God's people are at least called to "love one another." It seems reasonable, then, that I can expect more decent, more honest, more just, and more caring behavior from my brothers and sisters in Christ. Consequently, it does seem more offensive when fellow churchgoers treat me as badly or worse than anyone else does.

For me this issue is serious, as it often interferes with my worship of God. It is especially vexing to worship with the businessman who has recently cheated me out of a sum of money. In a pew nearby I sometimes see an extended family of established veterans, whose haughty eyes seem to say, "We've seen these preachers come and go, but we're the ones in charge here." I notice a man who asserts, "God is whatever you imagine Him to be." I sit next to a woman who considers the Bible a mere cultural artifact. Then perhaps there is the elder's wife, whose unrelenting gossip hurts so many people and tears at the fabric of the congregation. The list goes on, and there they all are singing the songs and saying the prayers along with everyone else.

In this homily Martin Luther speaks about the parable of the wheat and the tares, examining the perennial problem of counterfeit Christians in the church. As long as we live in this fallen world, says Luther, the church will have hypocrites and troublemakers worshipping among the true Christians. This is true for all denominations. Speaking of Jesus, Luther says:

> In this parable our dear Lord Jesus Christ advises us not to be offended when, as the word of the Gospel is sown, seeds of noxious tares are also sown among the good seed, so that as a result, bad and good, counterfeit Christians and genuine Christians, are mingled together....

His purpose, therefore, is to emphasize that whoever possesses the gospel should be forewarned and spiritually forearmed. For alongside the true, pure doctrine of the gospel many fanatical spirits, heresies, and offenses will sprout up, over which we must not fret unduly. (Fifth Sunday after Epiphany, vol. 1, p. 264)

To this comment Luther adds the picturesque maxim, "When God builds a church, the devil builds a chapel next door."

Luther acknowledges the great damage that is done by controversies in the church. To the world outside, these conflicts serve as a deterrent to any thoughts of wanting to be part of the church. Luther explains that when people who acknowledge the Christ publicly live as if Christ does not matter, "the gospel is scandalized before the world, turning people's eyes, ears, and hearts away from it" (266). Similarly, when teachers in the church teach and live contrary to the Gospel, "the scandalizing offense piles up" (266). Faith, fellowship, and joy are undermined; the devil seems to have the last laugh.

Further, Luther goes on to assert that contentious members within the church do more harm to the gospel than do its "avowed opponents and persecutors."

The parable makes it clear that placing problematic people in the church is certainly the work of Satan. With this fact in mind, Luther offers the following advice:

Therefore, be alert, be on your guard, and do not say, The field contains tares and, therefore, the field is worthless; or, because the field is dense with tares, no grain or wheat are present. No, you should rather say, The devil likes nothing better than to sow his tares among the wheat; and there is no one else whom he would rather trouble than true Christians. We must not hope or expect, therefore, that, just because the evangelical doctrine is good and completely in harmony, all who hear it will also be nicely united. Rather, things will proceed as before: mingled in with the wheat there will also be those who are not wheat, but tares. ...

> Everywhere, with but few exceptions, we find tares. Whoever wants to be a Christian will have to put up with his worst enemies calling themselves Christians and with finding false teachers and false Christians in the midst of orthodox teachers and Christians. (Fifth Sunday after Epiphany, vol. 1, pp. 267–68)

Luther reminds us not to over-react to false Christians among us, as there will always be some tares planted in every church.

My problem is that I have a natural impulse to distance myself from the obvious counterfeits. Some of them seem so smug at times, so full of pride as they spread their unkindness and trouble through the body of the church. In the past I kept changing churches in an effort to find a congregation without offensive people. Of course, I never did find the perfect one; this side of Heaven it doesn't exist. As part of the church, I realize that I, too, am the problem. I am far from perfect.

Luther reminds us that the early church under the apostles had many problem members to deal with, as the New Testament letters so clearly attest. Should we then expect to have it any better? Luther's homily is intended as encouragement to Christians who are deeply troubled by certain people in the church. Don't let them cause you to abandon the church, he says, because you will find more of them wherever you go.

Instead, we are urged to look beyond the tares and to appreciate the good wheat—those sincere, loving, persevering Christians who are still working hard despite the counterfeits in their midst. Luther says:

> We must ... learn correctly to identify the Christian church, and not to take offense when we see tares sprout and grow in the midst of the wheat.... (vol. 1, p. 268)

> "Let both grow together," says Christ, so that I retain my wheat, lest it be pulled out and destroyed; I shall ordain that at the proper time the reapers will gather up the tares so that they may be thrown into the fire. (Fifth Sunday after Epiphany, vol. 1, p. 276)

Luther's advice for people like me is twofold. First, he reminds me that I am far from flawless myself. I may in fact be a stumbling-block to another worshipper who knows all about my shortcomings. So my first duty is to humble myself and to pray for the Holy Spirit to guide me away from my own hypocrisy and troublemaking. I can pray daily, "Lord, make me wheat, and not a tare in my church."

Second, Luther says to look beyond the tares to see the real body of Christ. The parable of the wheat and tares is Jesus' clear message for me to stop my fussing about other people in the church; instead, to turn my attention and energies to the real work of the kingdom of God. Only in His forgiveness can I embrace my brothers and sisters in the faith. Only in His strength can I devote myself to the tasks He gives me.

Cherishing the Word

1. Why are there always false Christians in the church? What purpose do they serve?

2. Why does Luther say that conflicts within the church do more damage to the gospel than do the outsiders who reject and persecute the church?

3. What will be the outcome if we keep changing congregations in search of the "perfect church"?

> If nothing but corn and cockles and tares and no wheat were standing in the field, we might then trample and judge it to be useless. But since not only tares but also golden wheat are growing there, we must not reject it.... For the sake of the wheat, a Christian should value the field and not despise it because of the tares. (Fifth Sunday after Epiphany, vol. 1, p. 271)

• What encouragement can I take from Luther's assertion that the church will always be plagued with tares among the wheat?

• In my own church, have I done everything I can to prevent dissension, controversy, and hard feelings? Have I always put the peace and unity of the church before my own feelings and desires?

• What—specifically—can I say to myself whenever I am upset or bothered by certain other people in the church?

• What insights or blessings would I like to share with others?

> As a prisoner for the Lord, then, I urge you to live a life worthy of the calling you have received. Be completely humble and gentle; be patient, bearing with one another in love. Make every effort to keep the unity of the Spirit through the bond of peace. There is one body and one Spirit—just as you were called to one hope when you were called—one Lord, one faith, one baptism; one God and Father of all, who is over all and through all and in all. (Ephesians 4:1–6)

Reflections

12

WELCOMING THE
LORD'S SUPPER

*We welcome the Lord's Supper as God's gift
of forgiveness, comfort, and joy.*

Then came the day of Unleavened Bread on which the
Passover lamb had to be sacrificed. Jesus sent Peter and
John, saying, "Go and make preparations for us to eat
the Passover."

When do you want us to prepare for it?" they asked.

He replied, "As you enter the city, a man carrying a jar
of water will meet you. Follow him to the house that he
enters, and say to the owner of the house, 'The Teacher
asks: Where is the guest room, where I may eat the
Passover with My disciples?' He will show you a large
upper room, all furnished. Make preparations there."

They left and found things just as Jesus had told them.
So they prepared the Passover.

When the hour came, Jesus and His apostles reclined at
the table. And he said to them "I have eagerly desired to
eat this Passover with you before I suffer. For I tell you,

I will not eat it again until it finds fulfillment in the kingdom of God."

After taking the cup, He gave thanks and said, "Take this and divide it among you. For I tell you I will not drink again of the fruit of the vine until the kingdom of God comes."

And He took bread, gave thanks and broke it, and gave it to them, saying, "This is My body given for you; do this in remembrance of Me."

In the same way, after the supper He took the cup, saying, "This cup is the new covenant in My blood, which is poured out for you. (Luke 22:7–20)

As a child raised in the church, I grew up with a healthy respect for the importance and solemnity of the Lord's Supper. Looking back today, I recognize that my understanding of the sacrament was woefully meager. I had heard the warnings against partaking unworthily, and even as a youngster I possessed an intuitive sense that in the eating and drinking of the bread and wine something highly significant was taking place.

At the same time, I came to experience a habitual aversion to taking the elements of the Lord's Supper. During my teenage years this sense of dread became so pronounced that I would contrive ways to absent myself from the service whenever I saw the vessels waiting on the altar. I found these negative feelings troubling and I blamed myself for not having the pure heart that welcomes the sacrament as others seemed to do.

Martin Luther's excellent sermon on the institution of the Lord's Supper on Maundy Thursday is meant to instruct and encourage us about coming to the Lord's table even when our feelings may urge us to stay away. It was important to Luther that Christians should welcome the sacrament and participate in it with a sense of comfort and joy. It is, after all, the Lord's gift to His church.

The bread He proffers in His Body, and the cup or wine is His Blood, or the New Testament in His Blood. In childlike faith we should partake, without doubting, and believe it to be so. We should give thanks to Christ for such grace, rejoice over it, and strengthen our hearts by it, considering why Christ has done what He did, not disputing whether He is able to do it. (Holy Week, Maundy Thursday, vol. 1, p. 456)

There are two things, he says, that ought to make us want to participate in the Lord's Supper:

"First there's what we have to gain and what our need is, for Christ ordained and instituted the Sacrament for our benefit, comfort, and joy. Second, God's honor and glory ought to motivate us" (464). Beyond the great advantages the sacrament brings us, the benefit of giving honor and glory to God makes the sacrament even more important and worthwhile.

After his initial exposition clarifying the relationship between the Jewish Passover and the new Christian sacrament, Luther explains exactly what it is we proclaim when we participate in the Lord's Supper:

That is the service we render God in the New Testament … that when we receive the Sacrament, we proclaim with heart and mouth that Christ has shouldered our guilt and expunged our sin through the sacrifice of His Body and Blood. We ought to celebrate our Passover by extolling and praising the man who bears the name of Jesus Christ for His great, boundless redemption and for the everlasting kingdom and priesthood which He has won and granted us through His Body and Blood. He alone has conquered sin and death, in Himself, in His Body and Blood. And this is what He grants to us, and as a sure sign, pledge, and seal, He gives us His Body to eat and His Blood to drink in the Sacrament. (Holy Week, Maundy Thursday, vol. 1, p. 462)

In this sense we join together publicly to acknowledge and receive the gift of Jesus' sacrifice for our salvation. Here Luther adds, "whosoever receives the Sacrament thereby shows that he is expressing gratitude to Christ for His suffering and grace" (460).

Luther goes to great effort to refute the false doctrine that one must be blameless and free of sin in order to take the Lord's Supper properly. Readiness for the Lord's Supper lies not in our being sinless, but in our being repentant and truly believing His Word: "given for you, shed for you". We are to look upon the sacrament as our opportunity to get rid of our sins and be refreshed by the mercy of God. Luther continues:

> People who are conscious of their sins and sincerely desire to be rid of them should be urged to receive the Sacrament and not regard it as a judgmental occasion to be feared, but as welcome and comforting food for distressed souls.... Christians should be instructed to approach it with joy, confident and comforted, saying, I am a poor sinner, I need help and comfort, I wish to attend the Lord's Supper, and take nourishment from the Body and Blood of my dear Lord Jesus Christ. (Holy Week, Maundy Thursday, vol. 1, pp. 459–60)

I wish that someone had explained these things so clearly to me in my youth. Luther comes precisely to the point that it was my feelings of guilt and fear that kept me away from the Lord's Supper. Deep inside I always felt unworthy and I feared the grave consequences of simply going through the motions. These issues are indeed real and of great importance, but Luther explains that the sacrament does indeed provide a wonderful opportunity for me to get rid of my sins and receive the gifts of forgiveness, life, and salvation in Christ.

Seeing the sacrament in this way makes all the difference! I am released from bondage to my own sin and guilt, and this sense of redemption compels me to express my gratitude at the Lord's Supper. Thus, far from a dreaded or empty ritual, the sacrament becomes my opportunity to unload my sins and to proclaim my faith with the joy of one newly released from slavery. Yes, the sacrament is a solemn event, but it is solemn in the sense of a profound celebration. I now welcome the Lord's Supper in a spirit of gratitude and joy. As Luther notes, the Supper

> should not be a frightening experience for us but one of pure joy and laughter, particularly in the Spirit, so that we serve, praise, and give thanks to God for the grace and blessing shown us in Christ. For this reason we should willingly and happily go to the Sacrament, in all confidence saying, I, too, shall attend upon the true paschal lamb, and eat and drink of the Body and Blood of my dear Lord Jesus Christ, hold Him in remembrance, and thank Him for His redemption. (Holy Week, Maundy Thursday, vol. 1, p. 461)

The twofold benefits of the Lord's Supper are the comfort we receive and the honor we give to Jesus. Just as in the Passover the Jews gave thanks to God for their deliverance from bondage in Egypt, so in our sacrament do we give thanks to God for our salvation as well. Luther explains, "Therefore, when we partake of the Sacrament, we should give thanks to Him for His deliverance, not from Egypt and the Red Sea, but from sin, death, devil, hell, God's wrath, and every affliction" (461). In our thanksgiving we give honor to Christ for His work of grace, for as often as we eat and drink His body and blood, as Luther notes, our Lord is praised and honored by such remembrance and will receive our gratitude.

We should not dread the sacrament, nor should we let it become an empty ritual; for by it we are nourished in our faith, and our Lord Jesus Christ is honored in His holy Supper.

Cherishing the Word

1. In what way is the sacrament of the Lord's Supper similar to the Jewish Passover?

2. Luther says that we should not come to the Lord's Supper if we "love sin more than God's grace." Yet, he urges us not to let our sins drive us away from the comfort of the sacrament. How, then, can we prepare ourselves for the Lord's Supper?

3. What are the two important benefits of our coming to the Lord's Supper?

> Pay attention to His words and you will hear Him saying, I gave My life and shed My blood for you. He does not say that He gave His life and shed His blood in order to harm you; but He did this for you, for your benefit, to your comfort and strengthening, for the redemption of your soul, so that you might show more and more revulsion for sin, and more and more become a stronger Christian. (Holy Week, Maundy Thursday, vol. 1, p. 459)

• Do I sometimes let the Lord's Supper become a mere habit? What can I do to prevent it from becoming for me an empty ritual?

• When I see the table set for the Lord's Supper, what feelings come to me? In what ways can I grow to desire and appreciate the sacrament?

• What are some of the kinds of bondage from which I can celebrate my deliverance in Christ?

• What insights or blessings would I like to share with others?

> The Spirit of the Sovereign Lord is on Me, because the Lord has anointed Me to preach good news to the poor. He has sent Me to bind up the brokenhearted, to proclaim freedom for the captives and release from darkness for the prisoners, to proclaim the year of the Lord's favor. (Isaiah 61:1–2)

Reflections

Lord, Keep Us Steadfast in Your Word

Lord, keep us steadfast in Your Word;
Curb those who by deceit or sword
Would wrest the kingdom from Your Son
And bring to nought all He has done.

Lord Jesus Christ, Your pow'r make known,
For You are Lord of lords alone;
Defend Your holy Church that we
May sing Your praise triumphantly.

O Comforter of priceless worth,
Send peace and unity on earth;
Support us in our final strife
And lead us out of death to life.

—*Martin Luther (1542)*

13

BE READY FOR JESUS' RETURN

We remember that Judgment Day will indeed come unexpectedly, and in faith are ready for Jesus' promised return.

There will be signs in the sun, moon and stars. On the earth, nations will be in anguish and perplexity at the roaring and tossing of the sea. Men will faint from terror, apprehensive of what is coming on the world, for the heavenly bodies will be shaken. At that time they will see the Son of Man coming in a cloud with power and great glory. When these things begin to take place, stand up and lift up your heads because your redemption is drawing near.

He told them this parable: "Look at the fig tree and all the trees. When they sprout leaves, you can see for yourselves and know that summer is near. Even so, when you see these things happening, you know that the kingdom of God is near.

"I tell you the truth, this generation will certainly not pass away until all these things have happened. Heaven and earth will pass away, but My words will never pass away."(Luke 21:25–33)

Generally we don't like to think about death—particularly about our own. Indeed, we are told by psychologists that dwelling upon the thought of one's own death is a sign of a morbid and unhealthy personality. Yet for the Christian believer, there are few subjects more important to contemplate than that moment when we leave this mortal life on earth to enter the eternal adventure that lies beyond physical death.

In the human habit of avoiding the issue of death altogether, I have certainly been no exception. From those adolescent and teenage years when I simply considered myself indestructible, I grew into the routines and responsibilities of adult life—too busy to stop and think much about what might happen if I died today. The idea of Jesus' return is easy to relegate to a vague eschatological notion about some unknown epoch far in the future.

In his homily on Jesus' teaching on the Judgment Day at the end of time, Martin Luther urges Christians not to forget the Lord's promised return "with grandeur and majesty." Luther recognizes that the end of our time on earth is a subject we do not like to think about, and yet he says it is important always to keep this in mind.

The purpose of Jesus' prophecy about His return is to warn Christians against the kind of smugness and security that result from thinking that things will always go along just as they have in the past. Luther says:

> This is what the Lord proclaims in this Gospel: He cautions His Christians against becoming secure, so that the day of His coming might not come upon them unawares; He comforts them also so that they will not be terrified at the signs which will precede Judgement Day but rather rejoice that their redemption is drawing near. (Second Sunday in Advent, vol. 1, p. 38)

Luther offers both a warning and a comfort, grounded in the fact that Jesus will indeed return.

Luther warns us first not to imitate the ungodly and as Christians to keep in mind that "here in this life there is nothing enduring" (38). The world pours its efforts into the things of the world, but when the Day of Judgment comes, they will not be ready. Luther illustrates:

> For what will happen before Judgment Day is this: everybody will build, marry, surfeit, become secure, and in doing so burden their hearts, as if there were nothing else to do but that. Judgment Day will suddenly overtake these people who live this way, and Christ will come unexpectedly. When they are at their securest, when things rock with drumbeat, merriment, and dancing, they will suddenly be laid low and burn with a fire that will never be extinguished. (Second Sunday in Advent, vol. 1, p. 38)

In our times, we don't care for "fire and brimstone" sermons, and yet the truth is still the truth. Luther reminds us that the Judgment Day will come, even though fools may laugh at the very mention of it.

An important fact for Christians to keep in mind is that we shall be present at the Judgment Day—whether we live to see Jesus' second coming or we sleep in the grave awaiting this apocalyptic event. From a subjective point of view, that day will come suddenly for each one of us. Big Tent Revival, a popular Christian rock group, sings about being "only a breath away from your personal Judgment Day." These lyrics reflect Luther's point that each Christian lives in the conscious knowledge that Jesus' return is "only a breath away."

The warning here is that we must be careful not to fill our minds and hearts with concern about all the wrong things. Luther continues:

> The whole world will act secure. Don't let this disturb you, Christ admonishes, do not follow them; do not do what they are doing; cling to Me. Nor be afraid; keep your head high, and see to it that , when I come down from heaven, I shall be able to find you! Then you will experience no distress, for I shall come to deliver you. (Second Sunday in Advent, vol. 1, p. 40)

Luther explains that we "overload our hearts" when we put our hope in worldly things like becoming rich or famous or even simply comfortable. Speaking of those who are caught up in the commerce of the world, Luther explains:

> This is not to say that it is wicked and wrong to take nourishment, but as they go at it, they overload their hearts. Were they merely to put a burden on their hands, there would be no problem; for work is a necessity. But when they overload their hearts, that is what is evil and forbidden, namely, to put all their hope in becoming rich and famous. (Second Sunday in Advent, vol. 1, p. 40)

The pivotal questions are what our thoughts dwell upon and where we place our hopes.

During this past year I was given a clear reminder of my frail mortality. I celebrated Christmas day happily with my family, never once thinking about the possibility of my death. Within a few days, however, I was diagnosed as having a large cancerous tumor growing in my abdomen. It was a time of fear and uncertainty. There were tests and more tests to determine if the cancer had spread to the surrounding organs and bones. Even in my state of shock, I was fully aware that I might not survive the cancer or the surgery.

I saw clearly as never before the worthless distractions that cluttered my life and I understood my former sense of security as the illusion that it truly was. The issue of Jesus' return suddenly became much more than a theoretical event in the far future. I understood clearly the things that really matter: the hope of my Christian faith and my love for my wife and son.

The impending radical surgery was a frightful thing, but I prayed for God to release me from the grip of fear. The fear vanished and a profound sense of peace took its place. I was given the grace of knowing that, God would keep His promise whether I survived the cancer or not. I had nothing to fear.

In his sermon Luther balances his warning with lasting comfort. As we see the signs and as we watch and pray, we need not be frightened by the end times. Even when we witness all of those terrible signs and people's hearts are melting for fear, Luther says, "Lift up your heads and don't be afraid, for your redemption is drawing near." Luther paraphrases Jesus:

> When you see heaven and earth cracking apart, people more and more evil, and everything going out of joint, then be happy, be elated. About whom? About yourself? No, about Me, for I am coming; it will be a bit terrifying, for if I am to destroy the world, it will exhibit horror and turn our eyes. But I am there, be not afraid, you will be delivered. This we must keep in mind: we believe that our Lord Jesus Christ will assuredly come, and we shall have eternal life; however, just when this day and hour will come, we actually do not know; but we are pretty close to knowing, for the Lord says, "When these things begin to come to pass, then know that it is not far off." For this reason we must be ready, every day, every hour. (Second Sunday in Advent, vol. 1, pp. 42–43)

This message we cherish in our hearts and never forget, for no one knows when the end will come. We seek always to be ready.

How can we be ready? Luther replies, "If thus we accept warning, watch, and pray, we can then rest assured that Judgment Day will not terrify us" (42). Being ready for Jesus' return means not forgetting that Judgment Day will come, but it also means not being afraid or dreading the day. The way to be ready is to believe in Jesus Christ, to be baptized, and to pray daily. Luther concludes, "Therefore, we pray: Heavenly Father, let Thy kingdom come; deliver us from evil. Help, God, help, let Your might be felt in all directions, and make an end of all things" (42).

We are ready for our Lord. We truly believe that in the end our gracious Savior will indeed deliver us.

Cherishing the Word

1. "Fire and brimstone" preaching has gone out of fashion. Has the message of warning about God's judgement become obsolete? What happens to people who refuse to listen to God's warnings?

2. Luther says that people who "overload their hearts" with worldly matters are unprepared for Jesus' return. What are some of the ways we overload our hearts?

3. What can we do to be ready for Jesus' return and for Judgment Day?

> But let's listen to what Christ says, await His return, and pay no attention to what the ungodly and secure of the world are doing. For the Lord sincerely cautions us to look for His glorious return, because it is a sure thing. (Second Sunday in Advent, vol. 1, p. 39)

• What comfort can I gain from Christ's promise with regard to my faith and the flow of world events?

• Am I ready for Jesus' return? Can I truly rejoice at the thought of the end of time and the appearance of Jesus? Why, or why not?

• What fears and losses come to my mind when I contemplate the end? What are God's sure and eternal promises to me about these matters?

• What insights or blessings would I like to share with others?

> I love You, O Lord, my strength.
>
> The Lord is my rock, my fortress and my deliverer; my God is my rock, in whom I take refuge.
>
> He is my shield and the horn of my salvation, my stronghold.
>
> I call to the Lord, who is worthy of praise, And I am saved from my enemies. (Psalm 18:1–6)

Reflections